Let's Learn
Hindi

Web : www.jainbookagency.com
E-mail : sales@jba.in
Phone : 011-44556677

Let's Learn Hindi

Chaytna D. Feinstein

STERLING PAPERBACKS
An imprint of
Sterling Publishers (P) Ltd.
A-59, Okhla Industrial Area, Phase-II,
New Delhi-110020.
Tel: 26387070, 26386209; Fax: 91-11-26383788
E-mail: mail@sterlingpublishers.com
www.sterlingpublishers.com

Let's Learn Hindi
Copyright © 2004 by Deborah Feinstein
ISBN 978 81 207 2239 2
Reprint 2002
Revised Edition 2004
Reprint 2006, 2007, 2009, 2012

Printed in India
Printed and Published by Sterling Publishers Pvt. Ltd.,
New Delhi-110 020.

This book is dedicated to Swami Shyam.
India, its ancient wisdom, and its national language, all came
alive for me after meeting and hearing Swami Shyam speak in
both English and Hindi. Throughout the years, he has been
my constant inspiration, and my life has been immeasurably
enriched by his wisdom.

CONCEPT & RESEARCH BY THE AUTHOR

EDITOR-IN-CHIEF   Eric Myhr

ENGLISH EDITOR   Susan Cowan

COMPILATION   Zev Ordower

FORMATTING & LAYOUT DESIGN   Heidi Bornstein

COVER PAINTING   Stephen Aitken

GRAPHIC DESIGN   Ellen Reitman

BACK PHOTO   Raj Kamal Yadav

Acknowledgments

The dictionary defines *to acknowledge* as, 'to admit or accept the truth of a fact or situation,' and 'to express thanks for.' I would like to do both here.

The fact and truth is that none of the knowledge in this book could have come about without the enlightening presence of Swami Shyam in my life. The ability to live with joy and knowledge has come from his teachings. Though that is beyond the realm of thanks, I still thank him with all my heart.

My next acknowledgement is to Roma and Syd. They not only gave me life and my first language, they encouraged me to pursue knowledge, freedom, and happiness, even when it took me to the other side of the globe.

As my English editor says, this book evolved organically through many years of research, teaching, and thought. But the admissible fact is that it is the accumulated knowledge and genius of many people. It could not have been done without their assistance and support, and I would like to acknowledge them all.

First and foremost, I would like to thank Zev Ordower for his devoted help in compilation, research, and layout. He took on the arduous task of entering into the computer the lists of vocabulary, as well as the many revisions and additions.

Eric Myhr, the editor-in-chief, painstakingly laboured over the grammar sections, sculpting and coaxing the material into clear and concise text. It is due to his many hours of thought and consideration that this book now emerges as a cohesive and comprehensive whole.

My Hindi advisors have been invaluable. Alka Shrivastava was a special joy to work with. It was a privilege to dip into her great reservoirs of Hindi knowledge, and I thank her for the meticulous attention she gave to checking everything. Innumerable thanks also go to the other Hindi advisors and proofreaders, especially to Glen Kezwer PhD, who devoted hours of time and effort when it was most needed. Raj Kamal Yadav and Dan Ordower also added their expertise and attention to the Hindi text of this book.

Susan Cowan, the English editor, deserves great recognition for the tremendous job done with the English text and the grammatical information. It is fortunate for me that she is a kind neighbour and friend, never minding my round-the-clock, exhaustive inquiries. Thanks also to another dear friend and neighbour Jaanaca Chick, for her assistance in research and proofreading.

A large part of creation is in the manifestation, and this was accomplished through the computing and formatting skills of Heidi Bornstein. She spent many days and nights sorting through an unwieldy, constantly changing manuscript, and shaped it into a stable, user-friendly, and professional book. I want to specially thank her for her creativity, friendship, and love. Were it not for her hard work in all aspects of this production, none of us would be reading this book today.

It is an honour to have the work of Stephen Aitken, an artist whose illustrations in many publications of the Canadian government and the Smithsonian Institute have won numerous international awards, in this book. His generous donation of his watercolour 'Morning Bath in the Ganges,' for the front cover, and the chapter divider for 'Pronouns' have made the book itself a work of art. I thank him for the beauty of the cover and for his work on the chapter dividers of the book.

The covers and dividers were further enhanced by the computer expertise and design sense of Ellen Reitman, who transformed the original watercolour into the magnificent front cover. Great thanks are due to her as well for the design and layout of the back cover and chapter dividers, and especially for the generosity and patience needed to complete the many hours of printing.

I am also indebted to Jonathan Hoare, my publishing consultant, for his experience and knowledge and to Jarrett Astroff for all his technical help.

Special thanks also go to all my proofreaders and advisors in both languages: Chaitanya Prakash, Aparajita Narain, Rick Tunis, Shruti Prakaash, Bennett Johns, Nina Lehrman, and Kevin Harmer. And, as is said in Hindi, 'special, special' thanks to Raani Webster for proofreading, friendship, care, and for just listening.

With the assistance of John Davidson, Kim Burnham, Kevin Pitcairn, Ellen Rosenberg, S.K. Ghai, Mary McGugan, and Alan Chesick, this book has now been launched into its wider world. I thank them all.

Finally, to any and all that read **Let's Learn Hindi**, *Anayk Dhanyavaad*! Many Thanks!

Chaytna D. Feinstein
I.M.I, Kullu-175101
Himachal Pradesh

Introduction

Hindi is not difficult to learn, and this book will enable those with no previous knowledge of this language to reach a point where they can read, write, and converse in it.

Hindi is a rich and melodic language, spoken, written, and studied widely throughout India, both as a mother tongue and as a second or third language. Learning it will open the door to a fascinating and diverse culture that spans thousands of years of uninterrupted history.

The primary source of Hindi is Sanskrit, one of the most ancient spoken and written languages in the world, and one of the earliest ancestors of the Indo-European language family. Like Sanskrit, Hindi is written in the *Dev Naagari* script, which is common to several other Indian languages as well. Much of the vocabulary of Hindi comes from Sanskrit, though Hindi also has a special relationship with Urdu. Their grammar and much of their vocabulary are virtually identical, though Urdu is written in a modified form of the Arabic script.

Language is a natural and basic skill in a human being, and a child has an innate capacity to learn many languages. The potential must still exist within everyone, no matter what their age or training. It is just a matter of finding a method or system of getting the particular pattern of a language into the mind, and then getting that information to function.

I have been teaching Hindi to a growing group of people of all ages, languages and professions from all over the world. Because of the diversity of my students, I needed to find a method that was simple, immediate, and did not require too much memorization. This book evolved naturally from years of looking for a system which would assist anyone to acquire Hindi vocabulary and understand the elements of its grammar.

Out of my own experience of studying and teaching Hindi for over fifteen years, I developed the idea for a book with chapters arranged according to the parts of speech and their order in a Hindi sentence. This system proved to be a useful and quick way of finding the required word, even during conversations in progress with Hindi-speaking people.

Thus, I had all my students make their own books, following the pattern of this one. As their knowledge increased, they would add words and rules to their books, which they could then carry with them to practise their Hindi. Zev Ordower, a computer engineer from Montreal, Canada, experienced the efficacy of the handwritten book he created in our class. He then transferred all the data to a laptop computer, thereby enabling the idea to evolve further.

The Hindi presented in this book is primarily conversational, and is that which is used in all facets of formal and informal interaction by Hindi speakers and writers. Living and teaching in a Hindi-speaking part of India, I have been able to test, improve, and see the results of this method. People using this book have usually found, even after the first lesson, that they can converse simply with Hindi speakers, with the confidence that they are using the most appropriate word and correct sentence structure.

I have found **Let's Learn Hindi** to be an effective teaching and learning tool for both groups and individuals. People at all stages of learning Hindi have appreciated it as a continually useful source of reference and information and have found its method to be enjoyable and inspiring. I hope you have the same results.

Table of Contents

Chapter Contents

Adjectives

Nouns

Postpositions

Adverbs

Compound Verbs

Supplementary Notes

Conjunctions

Numbers

How to Use this Book

Let's Learn Hindi is designed in an easy and straightforward manner for students at all levels who wish to learn Hindi conversation and grammar.

While this book is sufficiently rich in vocabulary to be used as an English-Hindi dictionary by the student already familiar with Hindi, the organization of the book as a whole is intended to help those new to its study to begin to express in Hindi. To this end, the book begins with a complete course in the *Dev Naagari* (Hindi) script and subsequent chapters (Pronouns, Adjectives, Nouns, etc.), are arranged according to the order in which the words appear in a normal Hindi sentence.

Each chapter contains the necessary rules and a comprehensive English-Hindi dictionary for the part of speech discussed. For each English word listed in the dictionary, only the one or two Hindi words most commonly heard in conversation are given. If more than one word is given, either can be used.

To construct a full sentence in Hindi, move from chapter to chapter, taking words and grammar from each, until you reach the verb, which is usually found at the end of the Hindi clause or sentence. If you have begun by making a clause and wish to continue your sentence, choose the appropriate conjunction or linking structure, and repeat the same process until you finish the sentence. Following this process, the general order of any sentence will be correct.

The word order in a typical Hindi sentence is, for the most part, the reverse of that of the average English sentence. In an English sentence the subject of the sentence (i.e., the person or thing doing the action) appears first, then the verb (or action of the sentence), followed by its object(s).

1

However, in Hindi, the verb generally appears at the end of the clause or sentence, unlike English, where it is found near the subject of the sentence. In Hindi, the subject comes first, then the object(s), and finally the verb completes the clause or sentence.

Another notable difference between Hindi and English is that Hindi nouns are either masculine or feminine in gender, and any adjective describing a noun must agree in gender and number (singular or plural) with its noun.

An invaluable suggestion for those aspiring to speak Hindi with the naturalness and fluidity of a Hindi-speaking person is to try to keep your sentences simple. The Hindi sentence is built of small simple parts, linked to form compound structures (sentences that have more than one verb) using various types of conjunctions (e.g., and, or, but, if…then…, when…then…, etc.).

To give the reader a sense of how Hindi sentences are built, a list of sentences is given in which English words are arranged according to the positions they would occupy in a Hindi sentence. (See Sample Sentence Structures, pg. 6). Beginning with the simplest sentence structure, sentences of increasing complexity are formed with the addition of one new element at a time. You might find this chart helpful when constructing your first few Hindi sentences. Try building a number of sentences with the simpler structures and become comfortable with them before moving on to more complex structures. After becoming familiar with Hindi sentence structures, flip from chapter to chapter and start building your own sentences.

2

An informal description of grammatical terms can be found at the beginning of the book (see pg. 4). Readers unfamiliar with the language of grammar will find it useful to read this section over before attempting the rest of the book. Readers familiar with English grammar should note that some of the terms are specific to Hindi grammar.

The purpose of the arrangement of **Let's Learn Hindi**, is to make learning this language easy and immediate. Start using it and see the results!

Pronunciation of the Hindi sound system can be heard on an optional audio CD. For information on ordering the CD or for updates to this book, please visit the following web site:

www.letslearnhindi.com

Grammatical Terms

Adjective: A word used to describe a noun, specifying its size, quality, or quantity (e.g., big, nice, few).

Adverb: A word used to modify a verb, adjective, or another adverb, which describes the manner, extent, time, and location of the action (e.g., loudly, fully, soon).

Case: The form of a noun showing its function in the sentence. In Hindi there are two cases. A noun is said to be in the <u>oblique case</u> if it is followed by a postposition and is said to be in the <u>direct case</u> otherwise.

Clause: A clause is a group of words within a sentence that has its own subject and verb.

    Main Clause: A main clause can stand alone as a complete sentence.

    Relative Clause: An incomplete clause that is used with a main clause to express a related idea.

Conjunction: A word connecting two separate parts of a sentence (e.g., and, or, but, because). In Hindi adverbs are often used as conjunctions (e.g., therefore, rather, however, thus).

Intransitive: See **Verb**.

Noun: A name or word used for a person, place, or thing (e.g., book, temple, Delhi, Seeta). A noun can be the subject of a sentence or the object of a verb or a postposition.

Object: A noun, noun phrase, or pronoun that receives the action of a transitive verb or postposition.

    Direct Object: A noun, noun phrase, or pronoun that directly receives the action of the verb (e.g., 'apples' in 'Bring her the apples.')

    Indirect Object: A noun, noun phrase, or pronoun that indirectly receives the action of the verb (e.g., 'her' in 'Bring her the apples.')

4

Oblique Case: See **Case**.

Postposition: A word or words used to show the relation of a noun or pronoun to some other word in the sentence or clause (e.g., to, from, by, in). In English, these are called prepositions because they come before their object, but in Hindi they are called postpositions since they follow, rather than precede, the object.

Pronoun: A word used in place of a noun, to represent a person or thing (e.g., I, he, she, you, it, that, somebody).

Relative-Correlative Structure: A compound structure made up of a main clause and a relative clause. The relative clause contains a relative pronoun, adverb, or adjective, which functions as a sort of placeholder for a correlative pronoun, adverb, or adjective in the main clause.

Subject: A word or phrase used to represent the doer of an action (e.g., 'I' in 'I am running') or the one in a state of being or becoming (e.g., 'I' in 'I am happy').

Transitive: See **Verb**.

Verb: A verb expresses an action or a state of being or becoming of a thing (e.g., to do, to eat, to be, to happen).

> **Intransitive Verb:** A verb which does not take a direct object (e.g., 'Go' in 'Go quickly!').

> **Transitive Verb:** A verb which takes a direct object (e.g., in 'I do the work,' 'do' is transitive and the direct object is 'work').

Sample Sentence Structures

The simplest sentence:

SUBJECT	NOUN	VERB
I	**boy**	**am.**

Adding an adjective:

SUBJECT	ADJECTIVE	NOUN	VERB
Raam	**good**	**boy**	**is.**

Adding a new verb:

SUBJECT	ADJECTIVE	NOUN	VERB
He	**good**	**books**	**reads.**

Adding an adverb of manner:

SUBJECT	ADJECTIVE	NOUN	ADVERB	VERB
They	**good**	**books**	**quickly**	**read.**

Adding an adverb to express negation:

Adverbs of negation (e.g., not, never) are placed as close to the verb as possible.

SUBJECT	ADJECTIVE	NOUN	NEGATION	VERB
We	**bad**	**books**	**not**	**will read.**

Adding an adverb of time:

Adverbs of time or place may be placed at the beginning of the sentence, rather than near the verb.

SUBJECT	ADVERB	ADJECTIVE	NOUN	ADVERB	VERB
She	**later**	**good**	**books**	**quickly**	**will read.**

Using a postposition:

SUBJECT	NOUN	POSTPOSITION	VERB
I	**girl**	**to**	**speak.**

Adding a conjunction to make a compound sentence:

SUBJECT	NOUN	ADVERB	VERB	CONJUNCTION
I	**books**	**quickly**	**read**	**but**

SUBJECT	NOUN	ADVERB	VERB
you	**books**	**slowly**	**read.**

Using a conditional structure:

CONJUNCTION	SUBJECT	NOUN	VERB
If	**you**	**store**	**go**

CONJUNCTION	NOUN	VERB
then	**milk**	**buy.**

Using a relative-correlative structure:

RELATIVE	SUBJECT	NOUN	VERB
When	**we**	**store**	**go**

CORRELATIVE	SUBJECT	NOUN	VERB
then	**we**	**milk**	**will buy.**

Verbal constructions using को 'to':

LOGICAL SUBJECT	NOUN	VERB
To me	**happiness**	**is.**

Important Note

In Hindi, there is no introductory construction equivalent to 'there is/there are'. The English sentence 'There are girls here,' becomes, in Hindi, 'Girls are here.'

7

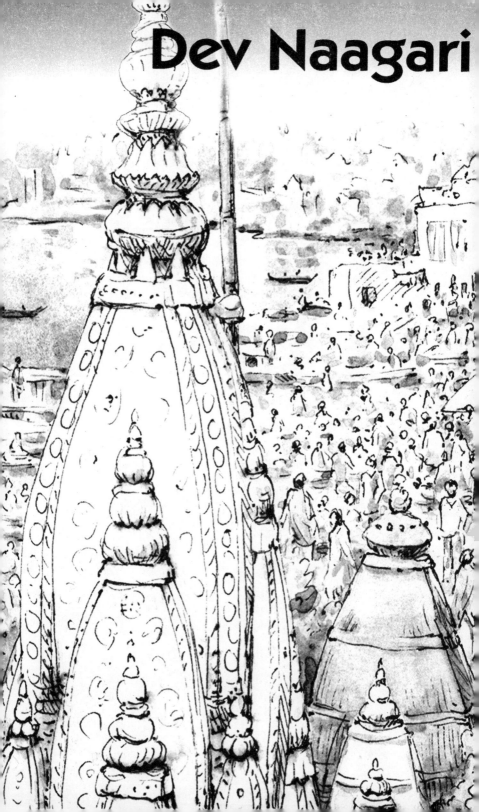

Dev Naagari

Dev Naagari
The Divine Language

Hindi is written in a script called *Dev Naagari*, which means sound arranged in such a way that divine consciousness, the highest awareness, is unfolded. The very words *Dev Naagari* mean divine language, where a person touches the inner field of resonance and sound, and reaches the climax of consciousness. This consciousness gives one the strength, energy, or power to understand what is best for human life.

First of all, a human being does not want to die! That is, each one wants to be immortal. Everyone knows that they are working in order to maintain their life for as long as possible. If they were given the choice, they would choose or wish to live forever. This consciousness, which wants to live forever, is found in every sentient being; therefore, it must be the truth. Why is it then, that everybody dies? Human beings work to save themselves from death, and in this way, pass their lifetime without reaching the goal of becoming immortal or undying, and, thereby, happy and at peace.

I would like to say that those who are capable of unfolding the divine consciousness, the immortal consciousness, from within, will find that the power that takes care of their body, mind, intellect, and ego-consciousness will also manifest from within. This power will make each person happy, peaceful, joyful, and capable of contributing to his or her children, friends, family, and world. The very *Dev Naagari* alphabet becomes the mantra— the advice or technique for easily unfolding the highest consciousness—provided one knows the truth of it.

All sounds come from one original sound: *mmmmmm*. This sound is neither Hindi nor Sanskrit, neither English nor French, nor Hebrew, nor any other language. It is the basis of all sounds.

9

The same sound then develops into *aaaaaahhhh*, which starts from the navel point and ends in silence—the field from where it emanated.

The arrangement of the sounds of *Dev Naagari* appeared from beyond: a *rishi*—or sage, or meditator—was sitting in silence, when a channel suddenly bubbled up, causing him to speak. Later on, several additions were made, but the original is from beyond.

Varn, or letter, means that indivisible sound that manifests and is heard. It is constructed with the help of the combined action of the palate, throat, tongue, and breath; for example, the sounds *a* or *ee* or *ka*. The sound of these letters cannot be divided in any way, but the letters can be put into two categories, vowels and consonants.

Vowels are those letters whose manifestation is not dependent on any other letter. No help from any other letter is needed to pronounce them. Therefore, the vowels in the Hindi or *Dev Naagari* script are arranged first:

अ a	आ aa	इ i	ई ee
उ u	ऊ oo	ऋ hri	
ए ay	ऐ ai	ओ o	औ ow
अं ang	अः aha		

There are two divisions of vowels: ordinary vowels and combined vowels. Ordinary vowels are those where the sound is spoken independently, such as a अ, i इ, u उ. However, long vowels are made by the combination of two sounds, such as:

$$a + a = aa \quad अ + अ = आ; \qquad i + i = ee \quad इ + इ = ई;$$
$$u + u = oo \quad उ + उ = ऊ; \qquad a + i = ai \quad अ + इ = ऐ;$$
$$a + u = o \quad अ + उ = ओ; \qquad a + o = ow \quad अ + ओ = औ.$$

There are three categories of vowel pronunciation:

1. *Hraswa* is the short sound. The vowel is pronounced with a very short sound, (e.g., अ **a**, इ **i**, उ **u**).

2. *Deergh* is a long sound. The vowel needs twice the pronunciation time of the short vowels, (e.g., आ **aa**, ई **ee**, ऊ **oo**, ऐ **ai**, औ **ow**).

3. *Plut* is when the pronunciation of the vowel is triple the time of the ordinary short vowel. This is not generally written in Hindi and is mostly seen in Sanskrit.

In pronouncing vowels, only the vocal chords are used. No other muscles that touch each other are put into play; everything takes place in the throat. Whoever begins learning the *Dev Naagari* script, using these sounds and vowels, will be able to unfold the highest awareness automatically. By repeating them, which is necessary for remembering the sounds, the human consciousness will attain a sense of freedom from its attachment to the body. Thus, even the vowels of *Dev Naagari* will transform the human consciousness into freedom and divinity.

We now proceed to the consonants, the second category of letters. Consonants are those letters that cannot be pronounced without the help of vowels, which means the sound of the vowel is necessary for pronouncing the consonant; for example, क **ka** or ध **dha** or प **pa**. Their pronunciation takes half the time of the vowels. Each consonant uses the sound of a vowel to be pronounced, and whatever type of vowel sound is needed is added to the consonant; for example, क् + अ = क, **k + a = ka**; क् + इ = कि, **k + i = ki**.

Halant is used when a consonant is pronounced without a vowel. It is a short diagonal mark moving downwards from left to right at the bottom of the written character. A *halant* indicates the absence of the vowel in the consonant (e.g., क्). If the *halant* is removed, the consonant immediately regains its original vowel sound, अ **a**, (क् + अ), and can be pronounced as क **ka**.

The consonants are arranged in five groups. In the first group the tongue is placed near the throat. In the second, the tongue is near the palate. In the third the tongue moves to the middle of the palate. In the fourth group, it is near the teeth. Finally it is on the lips. This is the order. It is as if you have drawn a semi-circle from the navel point right up to the lips. All five groups of consonants come from one point, one center, or *chakra*.

Now start the consonants:

The first group is **Gutteral** (base of throat):

क **ka**   ख **kha**   ग **ga**   घ **gha**   ङ **ang**

Here the throat is used in such a manner that we start from the navel point, come into the throat, and start using the throat muscles. The tongue is near the throat, and these five letters are pronounced from one point only.

The second group is **Pre-palatal** (beginning of palate):

च **cha**   छ **chha**   ज **ja**   झ **jha**   ञ **nya**

Here the tongue has moved to the middle of the palate. As we advance from the finest sounds to the grossest, the sound becomes more concretized with each group.

The third group is **Palatal** (middle of palate):

ट **ta**   ठ **tha**   ड **da**   ढ **dha**   ण **rna**

Here the tip of the tongue is curled, touching the top of the palate. All five are pronounced from the same place. If they are articulated in another way or from any other center, the pronunciation will be incorrect. [Dots appearing under letters indicate that they are palatal.]

The fourth group is **Dental** (teeth):

त ta   थ tha   द da   ध dha   न na

The tongue has now reached near the base of the lower teeth, or close to where the lower teeth start. The tongue should be touching the center between the gums and the teeth, and should touch the inside of the teeth while pronouncing these five letters.

The fifth group is **Labial** (lips):

प pa   फ pha   ब ba   भ bha   म ma

These consonants are pronounced with the lips.

[Charts for the alphabet, *maatraas*, and combination letters are found at the end of this section.]

At this point, I would like to repeat that the main purpose of learning *Dev Naagari* is not only to learn a language and the meaning therein, but rather to open a higher channel, a divine channel. The simplicity of the language is such that you can write each word exactly as you hear it; you do not have to memorize its spelling. For example, in English or in other languages, you often have to learn the joining of different letters by using a dictionary or by learning spelling from teachers. In *Dev Naagari*, once you have learned the vowels, consonants, and *maatraas* (the symbols of the vowels in combination with consonants), you will immediately be able to start writing and reading the script. After that, there remains only the work of repeating the script again and again, reading it, and, finally, picking up the meanings of the words, as they are found in the dictionary or with linguists. You have seen that it starts with the vowel अ **a** and ends with म **m**. Now the whole circle is completed.

The grammar is very simple because the subject comes first, then the object, and then the verb. Thus, it is very easy to learn, as this remains the basic order throughout. It is a simple grammar with simple combinations.

When you learn the Hindi language, you will find the beauty, the simplicity, and the joy that lies therein. No exertion is necessary to learn spelling; you can do it by yourself, though the basic sounds should also be heard. After that, a person can learn it all by himself and become a learned *pandit*, or master, one day.

Swami Shyam
Kullu, Valley of Gods, India

Notes on Writing the Script

All Hindi letters have a horizontal line covering them, with the exception of a few letters that show a break in the line. When writing Hindi letters, the covering line should be drawn after the letter, and its corresponding *maatraa* (if present), are completed, ensuring that the breaks are in the correct places. On lined paper, letters hang from the line above, rather than stand on the line below as they do in English.

The symbol for a period in Hindi is a 'stick' which appears at the end of sentences (e.g., मैं जाता हूँ। *Mai^n jaataa hoo^n*). The symbols '?' and '!' have been incorporated into Hindi, and are also used to close sentences.

Dev Naagari Alphabet

Vowels

अ	a	आ	aa	इ	i	ई	ee
उ	u	ऊ	oo	ऋ	hri		
ए	ay	ऐ	ai	ओ	o	औ	ow
अं	ang	अः	aha				

Consonants

	Unaspirated	Aspirated	Unaspirated	Aspirated	Nasal
Gutterals	क ka	ख kha	ग ga	घ gha	ङ ang
Pre-Palatals	च cha	छ chha	ज ja	झ jha	ञ nya
Palatals	ट ṭa	ठ ṭha	ड ḍa	ढ ḍha	ण rṇa
Dentals	त ta	थ tha	द da	ध dha	न na
Labials	प pa	फ pha	ब ba	भ bha	म ma
Semivowels	य ya	र ra	ल la	व va	
Sibilants	श sha	ष ṣha	स sa		
Glottal	ह ha				
Conjuncts	क्ष ksha	त्र tra	ज्ञ gya		
Fricatives	ख़ kha	ज़ za	फ़ fa		
Flaps	ड़ rḍa	ढ़ rḍha			

For full explanation, see Pronunciation Guide on page 20.

Maatraa-ay[n]

A *maatraa* is a symbol used for a vowel when it combines with (i.e., immediately follows) a consonant. The vowel अ 'a' is inherent in the basic form of all consonants (e.g., क ka, म ma, प pa); but by attaching a *maatraa*, the अ sound is replaced by a different vowel sound. Only one *maatraa* at a time may be attached to a consonant. If another vowel sound is to follow, it is written in its full form (e.g., कुआ *ku-aa*). The use of all *maatraas* is shown below with the consonant क्.[1] They combine with other consonants in exactly the same way (e.g., मा maa, पो po, etc.).

vowel	maatraa	combination	
अ		क् + अ = क	ka
आ	ा	क् + आ = का	kaa
इ	ि	क् + इ = कि	ki
ई	ी	क् + ई = की	kee
उ	ॖ	क् + उ = कु	ku[2]
ऊ	ॗ	क् + ऊ = कू	koo
ऋ	ृ	क् + ऋ = कृ	khri
ए	े	क् + ए = के	kay
ऐ	ै	क् + ऐ = कै	kai
ओ	ो	क् + ओ = को	ko
औ	ौ	क् + औ = कौ	kow
अं	ं	क् + अं = कं	kan(g)
अ:	:	क् + अ: = क:	kaha

---

[1] Note the use of the *halant* symbol (see pg. 11).

[2] The *maatraas* for उ and ऊ combine with the consonant र as: रु and रू.

Combination Letters

Combination letters are used when two consonants are pronounced without any vowel sound between them (e.g., as in the English word 'drip,' the 'd' and 'r' sounds are pronounced without any intervening vowel sound). Components of combination letters are joined in a number of ways. In some, the stem of the first letter is dropped and what remains is joined to the second letter:

प् + य = प्य (pya)   प्यार (*pyaar* 'love')

In others, part of the letter is removed and the remainder is attached to the second letter:

क् + ख = क्ख (kkha)   मक्खन (*mak-khan* 'butter')

Letters without a stem are combined in different ways; most are recognisable.

Some of the more unusually formed combination letters are shown below. Note the use of the *halant* symbol (see pg.11), which eliminates the inherent अ sound of consonants.

Letters	Comb. Letter	Example	Transliteration	English
क् + क = क्क		मक्की	*mak-kee*	corn
क् + त = क्त or क्त		मुक्त or मुक्त	*mukt*	free
क् + र = क्र		चक्र	*chakra*	wheel
क् + ऋ = कृ		कृष्ण	*Krishna*	Krishn
ट् + ट = ट्ट		मिट्टी	*mit-tee*	dirt
ट् + र = ट्र		राष्ट्रीय	*raashtreeya*	national

त् + त = त्त	कुत्ता	*kut-taa*	dog
त् + र = त्र or चित्र	चित्र or चित्र	*chitra*	picture
द् + द = द्द	गद्दा	*gad-daa*	cushion
द् + ध = द्ध	बुद्धि	*bud-dhi*	intellect
द् + म = द्म	पद्म	*padma*	lotus
द् + य = द्य	विद्या	*vidyaa*	wisdom
द् + र = द्र	चंद्र	*chandra*	moon
द् + व = द्व	विद्वान	*vidwaan*	scholar
द् + ऋ = दृ	दृश्य	*dhrishya*	scene
प् + र = प्र	प्रिय	*priya*	dear
प् + य = प्य	प्यार	*pyaar*	love
भ् + र = भ्र	भ्राता	*bhraataa*	brother
र् + म = र्म	धर्म / धर्मी	*dharm / dharmee*	duty / devout
र् + ण = र्ण	निर्णय	*nirnaya*	decision
श् + र = श्र	श्री	*shree*	Mr.
ष् + ठ = ष्ठ	गोष्ठी	*goshthee*	meeting
ष् + ट = ष्ट	व्यष्टि	*vyashti*	individual
ह् + म = ह्म	ब्रह्म	*brahm*	God
ह् + य = ह्य	गुह्य	*guhya*	secret

Notes on Pronunciation

In order to pronounce Hindi correctly, it is important to observe which vowel sounds are short and which are long. The length of each vowel plays a vital role in pronunciation, determining the rhythm of a word (see categories of vowel pronunciation, pg. 11).

Nasalization of certain sounds is a distinctive feature of Hindi, and words often show one of two symbols indicating that the letter below the symbol is nasal. A sound is made nasal by pronouncing the sound with the breath passing through the nose and constricting the throat slightly (as in honk and *bon vogage*). *Anusvaara* or *bindu* is a dot written over the nasalized letter to represent any one of the five nasal consonants (e.g., गेंद *gay[n]d* 'ball,' संभव *sa[m]bhav* 'possible'). The symbol called *chandra bindu* also denotes nasalization and is often used with letters that have no part of their symbol written above the line (e.g., आँख *aa[n]kh* 'eye,' हूँ *hoo[n]* 'am').

Aspirated consonants are pronounced with a definite exhalation, as if the consonant was combined with a following 'h' sound.

When the last letter in a word is a consonant, its inherent अ sound is often not pronounced unless it is a combination letter.

When the letter ह follows any other consonant, and neither ह nor the consonant has an attached *maatraa*, or vowel, then the अ 'a' sound in both letters is softened to an 'eh' sound, as in the words, 'red' and 'hen' (e.g., रहना is pronounced *rehenaa*).

Pronunciation Guide

Vowels

अ	a	as in b<u>u</u>tter
आ	aa	as in f<u>a</u>ther
इ	i	as in s<u>i</u>t
ई	ee	as in sl<u>ee</u>p
उ	u	as in p<u>u</u>t
ऊ	oo	as in m<u>oo</u>n
ऋ	hri	as in <u>ri</u>b
ए	ay	as in d<u>ay</u>[1]
ऐ	ai	as in s<u>ai</u>d
ओ	o	as in g<u>o</u>[1]
औ	ow	as in c<u>ow</u>
अं	ang	as in s<u>ung</u>[2]
अः	aha	as in <u>uh-huh</u>[3]

---

[1] These vowel sounds are diphthongs in English (i.e., composed of two vowel sounds; 'da-ee, go-u'). Only the first of these sounds is pronounced in the Hindi vowels described.

[2] *Anusvaara* or the dot written over letters, (see pg. 19) is illustrated here with the vowel अ 'a', but it can be used with any vowel or consonant (e.g. इं *ing*, हं *hum*).

[3] The symbol *visarga* resembles a colon, and is pronounced as a slightly aspirated echo of the preceding vowel sound. It can be used with any vowel, though it is most often found with अ 'a'.

Consonants

क	ka	as in <u>k</u>eep
ख	kha	aspirated form of क [4]
ग	ga	as in <u>g</u>arden
घ	gha	aspirated form of ग
ङ	ang	as in d<u>ung</u>
च	cha	as in <u>ch</u>art
छ	chha	aspirated form of च
ज	ja	as in <u>j</u>ar
झ	jha	aspirated form of ज
ञ	nya	as in e<u>n</u>joy
ट	ṭa [5]	as in s<u>t</u>and (see: Palatal, pg. 12)
ठ	ṭha	aspirated form of ट
ड	ḍa	as in <u>d</u>ark (see: Palatal, pg. 12)
ढ	ḍha	aspirated form of ड
ण	rṇa	as in Kris<u>hn</u>a (see: Palatal, pg. 12)
त	ta	as in <u>t</u>eeth (see: Dental, pg. 13)
थ	tha	aspirated form of त
द	da	as in <u>d</u>eal
ध	dha	aspirated form of द
न	na	as in <u>n</u>oble

---

[4] Recall that aspirated letters are pronounced with more breath exhaled, as if combined with a following 'h' sound.

[5] Dots appearing under letters indicate that they are palatal.

प	pa	as in park
फ	pha	aspirated form of प
ब	ba	as in bark
भ	bha	aspirated form of ब
म	ma	as in malt
य	ya	as in yacht
र	ra	as in raw
ल	la	as in large
व	va[6]	
श	sha	as in shark
ष	sha	palatal form of श
स	sa	as in salt
ह	ha	as in harp
क्ष	ksha	as in suction (combination letter क् + श)
ज्ञ	gya	as in egg-yolk combination letter ज् + ञ, but pronounced 'gya')
त्र	tra	as in trolley (combination letter त् + र)
ख़	kha	ख made with a scraping sound at the back of the throat.
ज़	za	as in zebra
ड़	rda	the palatal ड pronounced with a slight 'r' sound in the beginning.
ढ़	rdha	aspirated form of ड
फ़	fa	as in farmer

---

[6] This consonant is between the English 'w' and 'v' sounds. To pronounce it form the lips to pronounce 'v' but say 'wa' without rounding the lips.

Pronouns

A pronoun is a word that is used in place of a noun, to represent a person or thing (e.g., I, he, she, you, it, that). Pronouns have many forms in Hindi depending on their function in the sentence. When a pronoun is the subject of a sentence or clause it appears in the direct case (and influences the conjugation of the verb). When a pronoun is not the subject then it is in one of three other forms: when it is the object of a simple postposition it takes the oblique form (e.g., मुझसे 'from <u>me</u>'); when it is the object of a verb it is in the objective form (e.g., वह मुझे देखता है । 'He sees <u>me</u>'); when it shows ownership it takes the possessive form (e.g., मेरा नाम '<u>my</u> name').

Note that in Hindi the same pronoun, वह, is used for 'he,' 'she,' 'it,' and 'that.' Often the form of the verb and/or the context of the sentence will be the only indications of the gender of the subject and whether or not it is animate.

Sometimes the pronouns यह (this) and ये (these) are used instead of वह (he, she, it, that) and वे (they, those) respectively, when the person(s) or thing(s) referred to are in close proximity to the speaker.

Honorific Use of Pronouns

Hindi attributes different honorific values to its pronouns, which should be noted carefully. The pronouns तू, तुम, and आप all mean 'you.' तू is used when expressing intimacy and/or feelings of contempt or disgust, and should not be used by someone not perfectly at home in Hindi. तुम is used in situations of familiarity (e.g., between close friends and family members). The respectful pronoun आप is formal and polite in tone. Its use is recommended for those new to the language.

When referring to someone respectfully or formally in the third person, the plural pronoun वे should be used instead of वह:

वे मेरी माता-जी हैं ।   She is my mother.

Possessive Pronouns

Possessive pronouns agree in gender and number with the object that is being possessed, not with the possessor of the object. Regardless of who possesses the object, the possessive pronoun will agree with the object. For each possessive pronoun listed, three forms are given, corresponding to whether the object is masculine singular, feminine singular or plural, or masculine plural:

मेरा   masculine singular

मेरी   feminine singular or plural

मेरे   masculine plural

In the following examples, the nouns are assumed to be in the direct case:

मेरा कमरा my room (कमरा is a masculine singular noun.)

मेरा will be used whether the room belongs to a male or female. Any other possessive pronoun used with कमरा will also be in the masculine singular form (i.e., तुम्हारा कमरा, तेरा कमरा, etc.).

मेरी किताब my book   (किताब is a feminine singular noun.)

मेरी किताबें my books   (किताबें is the plural of किताब.)

मेरे कमरे   my rooms   (कमरे is the plural of कमरा.)

When the object of a possessive pronoun is a masculine singular noun followed by a postposition (and therefore in the oblique case), the ए ending is used instead of the आ ending (i.e., मेरे is used instead of मेरा, तुम्हारे instead of तुम्हारा, etc.):

मेरे घर में   in my house   (घर is a masculine singular noun.)

Pronouns with Postpositions

Just as the English pronoun 'I' becomes 'me' when governed by a preposition, so in Hindi a pronoun governed by a postposition changes its form. A pronoun can take one of several forms depending on the postposition. With simple postpositions, pronouns take the form given under Oblique; with compound postpositions, pronouns take the form given under Possessive (see Forms of Pronouns, pg. 27). A few of the commonly used postpositions with pronouns are listed on page 28. Notice that some postpositions are joined to the pronoun and are written as one word.

Alternate Forms of Pronouns with को

The oblique forms of pronouns with को (i.e., मुझको, उसको, तुमको, etc.) are equivalent to and interchangeable with the objective forms (i.e., मुझे, उसे, तुम्हें, etc.), and both forms mean 'me,' 'him,' 'you,' etc. The objective form is more commonly used and is always preferred when को appears elsewhere in the same sentence or clause.

Reflexive Pronouns

The reflexive pronoun अपने आप 'one's own self' is used for the English 'myself, yourself, himself,' etc., when followed by a postposition (usually को - see page 90 for further explanation on the use of को).

> भक्ति नाथ अपने आप को एक बड़ा लेखक समझता है । Bhakti
> Naath considers <u>himself</u> a great writer.
> क्या आप अपने आप को शीशे में देखते हैं ?
> Do you see <u>yourself</u> in the mirror?

Without a postposition अपने आप has an adverbial sense and means 'automatically' or 'of one's own accord':

25

वह सात बजे अपने आप उठ जाता है ।	He gets up <u>automatically</u> at seven o'clock.
उन्होंने अपने आप यह काम किया ।	They did this work <u>of their own accord</u>.

खुद and स्वयं also mean 'one's own self', but are mostly used in contexts in which they are not followed by a postposition. The emphatic ही is very often used with these reflexive pronouns:

वह स्वयं (<u>ही</u>) जा सकता है ।	He <u>himself</u> can go.
हम <u>खुद</u> (ही) यह काम नहीं करते ।	We don't do this work <u>ourselves</u>.

Possessive Adjective अपना 'one's own'

The possessive adjective अपना must be used when the object being possessed belongs to the subject of the sentence or clause. It agrees with its object in the same way possessive pronouns do:

मैं <u>तुम्हारा</u> खाना खाता हूँ ।	I eat <u>your</u> food.
but मैं <u>अपना</u> खाना खाता हूँ ।	I eat <u>my</u> (own) food
वह <u>तुम्हारी</u> किताब पढ़ता है ।	He reads <u>your</u> book.
but वह <u>अपनी</u> किताब पढ़ता है ।	He reads <u>his</u> (own) book.

When the object of अपना is a masculine noun followed by a postposition (and in the oblique case), अपने is used instead of अपना :

अपने घर में in one's own house

अपना is sometimes preceded by a possessive pronoun (मेरा, उसका, हमारा, etc.) to emphasize ownership:

यह <u>मेरी अपनी</u> कहानी है ।	This is <u>my own</u> story.
यह <u>उसका अपना</u> घर है ।	This is <u>his own</u> house.

Forms of Pronouns

Direct

Singular

I - मैं

you - तू

he, she, it, that - वह

this - यह

Plural

we - हम

you - तुम

you - आप

they - वे

these - ये

Oblique

Singular

me - मुझ

you - तुझ

him, her, it, that - उस

this - इस

Plural

us - हम

you - तुम

you - आप

them, those - उन

these - इन

Possessive (see pg. 24)

my - मेरा, मेरी, मेरे

your - तेरा, तेरी, तेरे

his, hers, its - उसका, उसकी, उसके

his, hers, its - इसका, इसकी, इसके

our - हमारा, हमारी, हमारे

your - तुम्हारा, तुम्हारी, तुम्हारे

your - आपका, आपकी, आपके

their - उनका, उनकी, उनके

their - इनका, इनकी, इनके

Objective

me - मुझे

you - तुझे

him, her, it, that - उसे

this - इसे

us - हमें

you - तुम्हें

you - आपको

them, those - उन्हें

these - इन्हें

27

Pronouns with Postpositions

With को 'to' (see pg. 25)

to me - मुझको

to you - तुझको

to him, her, it, that -
उसको

to this - इसको

to us - हमको

to you - तुमको

to you - आपको

to them, those - उनको

to these - इनको

With से 'by, from'

by, from me - मुझसे

by, from you - तुझसे

by, from him, her, it, that -
उससे

by, from this - इससे

by, from us - हमसे

by, from you - तुमसे

by, from you - आपसे

by, from them - उनसे

by, from these - इनसे

With में 'in' and पर 'at/on'

in, at/on me - मुझमें, मुझ पर

in, at/on you - तुझमें, तुझ पर

in, at/on him, her, it, that -
उसमें, उस पर

in, at/on this - इसमें, इस पर

in, at/on us - हममें, हम पर

in, at/on you - तुममें, तुम पर

in, at/on you - आपमें, आप पर

in, at/on them - उनमें, उन पर

in, at/on these - इनमें, इन पर

With के लिए 'for'
(see Postpositions pg. 86)

for me - मेरे लिए

for you - तेरे लिए

for him, her, it, that -
उसके लिए

for this - इसके लिए

for us - हमारे लिए

for you - तुम्हारे लिए

for you - आपके लिए

for them - उनके लिए

for these - इनके लिए

With ने

This form is used only in the Perfect Tenses.
(see Verbs pg. 113)

I - मैंने

you - तूने

he, she, it, that - उसने

this - इसने

we - हमने

you - तुमने

you - आपने

they - उन्होंने

these - इन्होंने

Possessive Adjective

one's own - अपना (see pg. 26)

Reflexive

one's own self - अपने आप, स्वयं, खुद, (see pg. 25)

Indefinite

all - सब

any - कोई

anybody else - कोई और

anyone - कोई भी

even some - कुछ भी

everyone - हर कोई

everything - सब कुछ

whoever - जो कोई

hardly anyone - कोई ही

no one, nobody - कोई नहीं

nothing - कुछ नहीं

some, somebody, someone - कोई (oblique - किसी)

somebody - कोई व्यक्ति

somebody else - कोई दूसरा, कोई और

someone or other - कोई न कोई

something - कुछ

something else - और कुछ

some more - कुछ और

something or other - कुछ न कुछ

somewhat - कुछ कुछ

whatever - जो कुछ

Relative[1]
the one(s) who, which, that - जो

Oblique Relative
to the one who, which, that - जिसे, जिसको

to the ones who, which, that - जिन्हें, जिनको

Interrogative
what - क्या [2]

which - कौन-सा [3]

who - कौन (oblique - किस)

---

[1] See Conjunctions pg. 168

[2] क्या must be placed after the first word of the sentence or clause. If it is in the first position, it conveys 'Do you,' 'Does he/she,' etc. or 'Is it/there,' 'Are there,' (e.g., क्या यह तैयार है? 'Is it ready?').

[3] कौन-सा agrees with its object in the same way possessive pronouns do.

Adjectives

An adjective is a word used to describe a noun, that is, its quality, quantity, etc. Generally adjectives precede the word they are describing (e.g., सुन्दर लड़की 'a <u>beautiful</u> girl'), but not always. When an adjective follows its object, the adjective is subtly emphasized (as in, यह लड़की <u>सुन्दर</u> है । 'This girl is <u>beautiful</u>').

An adjective ending in आ (e.g., बड़ा 'big,' अच्छा 'good') agrees in gender and number with the noun it is describing in the same way that possessive pronouns do.

All other adjectives (e.g., सुन्दर 'beautiful,' लाल 'red') are invariable (i.e., show no changes in spelling regardless of the gender and number of the noun they describe).

Agreement of Adjectives ending in आ

The agreement of these adjectives with nouns in the direct case (nouns not followed by a postposition) is illustrated in the following:

अच्छा	good
अच्छा कमरा	a good room (masc. sing.)
अच्छी किताब	a good book (fem. sing.)
अच्छे कमरे	good rooms (masc. pl.)
अच्छी किताबें	good books (fem. pl.)

When an adjective describes more than one person, then it shows the masculine plural ending, unless <u>all</u> the people are female, in which case the feminine ending is used:

अच्छे लड़के और लड़कियाँ	good boys and girls
but अच्छी महिलाएँ और लड़कियाँ	good women and girls

When an adjective describes more than one inanimate object, then it agrees with the nearest noun:

ये थालियाँ और प्याले गन्दे हैं । These plates and cups are dirty.

ये थालियाँ (f.pl.) और प्याले (m.pl.) गन्दे (m.pl.) हैं ।

Agreement with Oblique Case Nouns

When a masculine singular noun is followed by a postposition (and therefore is in the oblique case), the आ ending of the adjective changes to ए:

अच्छा आदमी	a good man (direct case)
but अच्छे आदमी को	to a good man (oblique case)

Endings of adjectives agreeing with feminine nouns or masculine plural nouns do not change in the oblique case (i.e., they are the same as in the direct case):

अच्छी किताब में   in a good book (oblique)

Adjectives not ending in आ
(all other adjectives)

These adjectives are invariable; that is, they show no change in spelling regardless of the gender, number, or case of their object:

सुन्दर	beautiful
सुन्दर कमरा	a beautiful room (masc. sing.)
सुन्दर किताब	a beautiful book (fem. sing.)
सुन्दर कमरे	beautiful rooms (masc. pl.)
सुन्दर किताबें	beautiful books (fem. pl.)
सुन्दर किताब में	in the beautiful book (oblique)

32

Making Comparisons

In Hindi, there are almost no comparative adjectives (e.g., bigger, hotter). Instead, the adjective in its positive (normal) form is used, (e.g., big, hot). The postposition से is used to compare two things; से follows the thing with which the comparison is being made:

महाबीर हनुमान से बहादुर है ।	Mahaabeer is <u>braver than Hanumaan</u>.
सीता मुझसे छोटी है ।	Seeta is <u>smaller (younger) than me</u>.[1]
यह फ़िल्म उस फ़िल्म से और दिलचस्प है ।	This film is <u>more interesting than that film</u>.

Adjectives are preceded by सबसे to express the superlative degree (e.g., सबसे अच्छा 'best', सबसे सुन्दर 'most beautiful'):

वह फ़िल्म सबसे अच्छी है ।	That film is <u>the best</u>.
अल्का सबसे सुन्दर लड़की है ।	Alka is the <u>most beautiful</u> girl.
बबलू सबसे बड़ा बेटा है ।	Babaloo is the <u>eldest (biggest)</u> son.
यह सबसे खराब उदाहरण है ।	This is <u>the worst</u> example.

When an object of comparison is not explicit, और 'more,' और भी 'even more,' and कम 'less' can precede an adjective to give it a comparative sense:

यह कम्बल और भारी है ।	This blanket is <u>heavier</u>.
वह कम्बल और भी भारी है ।	That blanket is <u>even heavier</u>.
यह साड़ी कम सुन्दर है ।	This sari is <u>less beautiful</u>.

---

[1] In comparative expressions, छोटा and बड़ा can also mean 'younger' and 'older' respectively.

33

The Suffix सा

सा is sometimes added to the end of an adjective (by means of a hyphen) where it has the effect of reducing or diffusing the sense of the adjective. Compare the following:

लाल	red	लाल-सा	reddish
अच्छा	good	अच्छा-सा	somewhat good
थोड़ा	little	थोड़ा-सा	just a little

Note that both सा and the adjective to which it is attached agree with the noun being described:

थोड़ी-सी चाय	just a little chai
लाल-से कपड़े	reddish clothes

सा may also be added to nouns and pronouns to form adjectives; in this usage सा means 'like' or 'similar to':

गाय	cow	गाय-सा	cow-like
लोमड़ी	fox	लोमड़ी-सा	fox-like
दिल्ली का सा तापमान			temperature like Delhi's
उसके-से कपड़े			clothes like his

A

a lot - बहुत, ज़्यादा

abstract - भाव वाचक

accurate - सही

acidic - खट्टा

active - फुर्तीला

additional - और

advanced - आगे बढ़ा हुआ

adventurous - साहसिक

affectionate - स्नेही

aged - बुज़ुर्ग

alert - सचेत, चुस्त

alive - ज़िन्दा, जीवित

all - सब, सारा

all right - ठीक

amazing - अद्भुत, आश्चर्यजनक

amusing - मज़ेदार, मनोरंजक

angry - नाराज़, क्रोधित

animated - सजीव

another - दूसरा, एक और

any - कोई

any other - कोई और

appropriate - उचित

approved - पसन्द

arrested - गिरफ़्तार

arrogant - गुस्ताख़, अहंकारी

artificial - नक़ली

ashamed - शर्मिन्दा, लज्जित

assembled - एकत्रित

astonished - भौचक्का, विस्मित

athletic - कसरती

atomic - अणुकण

attractive - आकर्षक, मोहक

auspicious - शुभ

authentic - प्रमाणित

available - मौज़ूद

average - मध्य

awakened - प्रबुद्ध, जागृत

awful - भयंकर, बहुत ख़राब

awkward (clumsy) - भद्दा

B

back - पिछला

backwards - उल्टा

bad - ख़राब, बुरा

bad mannered - बदतमीज़

bad tasting - बदमज़ा

balanced - सन्तुलित

bald - गंजा

barren - बंजर

beautiful - सुन्दर, ख़ूबसूरत

beloved - प्यारा

best - सबसे अच्छा, श्रेष्ठ

better - बेहतर

bewildered - व्याकुल

big - बड़ा

black - काला

blessed - धन्य

blind - अन्धा

blissful - आनंदित, आनंदमय

blue - नीला

bold - दिलेर, साहसी

both - दोनों

both sides - दोनों ओर

bound - बन्द

brass - पीतल

brave - बहादुर, बलवान, साहसी, वीर

brief - संक्षिप्त

bright - चमकीला

brilliant - नूर

broken (in pieces) - पाश

brown - भूरा

busy - व्यस्त

C

calm - शान्त

canceled - मंसूख, स्थगित

capable - समर्थ, लायक

careful - सावधान

careless - असावधान,

catastrophic - विनाशकारी

celebrated - मशहूर, प्रसिद्ध

central - मध्य

certain - पक्का

certain (things) - कुछ ही (चीज़ें)

charitable - दयालु, कृपालु

charming - आकर्षक

cheap - सस्ता

childish - बचकाना

childlike - शिशु-सुलभ, बाल-सुलभ

clean - साफ

clear (lucid) - स्पष्ट·

clever - चतुर, चालाक

close (intimate) - जिगरी

closed - बन्द

clumsy - भद्दा

coincidental - इत्तफ़ाक़ी

cold - ठण्डा

collected - जमा, एकत्रित

colorful - रंगीन

colorless - बेरँग, रंगहीन

comfortable - आरामदायक

common - सामान्य, साधारण

communicable - संचारी

completely - ﾟबिलकुल

conceited - घमंडी

concrete (tangible) - मूर्त, ठोस

confused - संभ्रान्त

constant - निरन्तर, लगातार

contagious - संक्रामक

contained - निहित

continuous - लगातार

convenient - सुविधाजनक

cool - शीतल

costly - महँगा

countless - अनगिनत, कोटि

courageous - दिलेर, साहसी

courteous - तमीज़दार

cowardly - भीरु, कायर

crazy - पागल, सनकी

criminal - मुजरिम

crooked - कुटिल, टेढ़ा

cruel - क्रूर, निर्दय

cunning - चालाक

curious - जिज्ञासु

curly - घुँघराला

current - प्रचलित

D

damp - नम, गीला

dangerous - खतरनाक

dark - अँधेरा

dear - प्रिय, प्यारा

dearest - प्रियतम

deceitful - प्रपंची, कपटी, छली

decent - शरीफ़

deep - गहरा

dejected - उदास

delicious - स्वादिष्ट, लज़ीज़

delighted - प्रफुल्ल, आनंदित

dense (thick) - घना

dependent - निर्भर

deserving - अधिकारी

destitute - दीन-हीन, अकिंचन

devout - धर्मी

different - भिन्न, और

difficult - कठिन, मुश्किल

direct - सीधा

dirty - गन्दा

disappeared - गायब, विलीन, अदृश्य

disciplined - अनुशासित

discourteous - बदतमीज़

discriminating - विवेकशील

disgraced - अपमानित, बदनाम

dishonest - बेईमान

disloyal - नमक हराम

displeased - नाराज़

divine - दिव्य, ईश्वरीय

domestic - पारिवारिक, घरेलू

doubtful - संदिग्ध, संदेहयुक्त

dry - सूखा

dumb (mute) - गूँगा

durable - टिकाऊ

dynamic - शक्तिमान, शक्तिशाली

E

each - हर, प्रत्येक

eager - आतुर, उत्सुक

eastern - पूर्व

easy - सहज, आसान

eccentric - झक्की, सनकी

efficient - दक्ष, कुशल

eldest - सबसे बड़ा

elegant - मनोरम, ललित

emotional - भावुक

empty - खाली

empty-handed - खाली हाथ

energetic - फुर्तीली, कर्मठ

enjoyable - मज़ेदार

enlightened - प्रबुद्ध

enough - काफ़ी

entire - तमाम, सारा, समस्त

equal - समान, बराबर

established, firm - स्थापित, दृढ़

eternal - शाश्वत, सनातन,
अनन्त, नित्य

ethereal - आकाशीय

even - बराबर, समतल, सम,
एक-सा

every - हर, प्रति, प्रत्येक, हर एक

exact - सही, बिल्कुल, ठीक

excellent - सर्वश्रेष्ठ, सर्वोत्तम

exciting - उत्तेजक

expensive - कीमती, मूल्यवान,
महँगा

experienced - अनुभवी

expert - कुशल

exquisite - उत्कृष्ठ

exterior - बाहरी, बाह्य

extra - अतिरिक्त

extraordinary - असाधारण

extreme - अति, अत्यन्त

F

faint - फीका, हल्का

fair (colored, white) - गोरा

fair (honorable) - ईमानदार

faithful - विश्वसनीय

fake - नकली

familiar - परिचित

famous - प्रसिद्ध, प्रतिष्ठित

far - दूर

far enough - काफी दूर

fast - जल्दी, शीघ्र

fat - मोटा

favorite - मन पसन्द

feminine - स्त्रीलिंग, स्त्रैण

few - कुछ

fierce - प्रखर, उग्र

finished - समाप्त, सम्पूर्ण, खत्म

first - पहला

flowering - पुष्पित

flowing - बहता हुआ

fluent - प्रवाहित

foolish - मूर्ख, बुद्धू, बेवकूफ

forbidden - मना

foreign - विदेशी

free - स्वतंत्र, मुक्त

free (of charge) - मुफ़्त

fresh - ताज़ा

friendly - हितैषी, हितकारी,
मिलनसार

frustrating - बेबस

full - पूरा, पूर्ण, भरा

funny - मज़ाकिया, हास्यप्रद

G

general - आम, साधारण, सब का, सर्वजनिक

generous - उदार, दयालु, कृपालु

gentle - भला, शरीफ़, नम्र

genuine - असली

glad - खुश, प्रसन्न

glittery - जगमग

golden - सुनहरा

good - अच्छा

gradual - आहिस्ता

grand - शानदार

grateful - आभारी, कृतज्ञ

gratified - कृतकृत्य

gray - सलेटी

great - महान

greedy - लालची, लोभी

green - हरा

grumpy - चिड़चिड़ा

H

half - आधा

half (number) - साढ़े

handsome - खूबसूरत

haphazard - गड़बड़

happy - प्रसन्न, सुखी, खुश

hard - सख्त

hardly (a few) - कुछ ही

hazy - धुँधला

healthy - तंदुरुस्त, स्वस्थ

hearty, heartfelt - हार्दिक

heavy - भारी

helpless - विवश, बेकार, मज़बूर

high - ऊँचा

historical - ऐतिहासिक

holy - पवित्र, पुनित

honest - ईमानदार

honorable - मान्य

hot - गरम

huge - लंबा-चौड़ा

human - मानवीय

humid - गीला

hygienic - स्वास्थ्यकर, साफ़-सुथरा

I

idle - निठल्ला

illegal - अवैध

illiterate - अनपढ़

immature - अपक्व, अपरिपक्व

immortal - अमर

imperfect - अपूर्ण

important - महत्वपूर्ण, ज़रूरी

impossible - असंभव

impractical - अव्यवहारिक

impressive - प्रभावशाली

improper - अनुचित

impure - अशुद्ध

inactive - निष्क्रिय

inadequate - अपर्याप्त

inanimate - निष्प्राण, जड़, अचेतन

inauspicious - मनहूस, अशुभ

incapable - असमर्थ

incomparable - अनुपम

incompetent - अशक्त, अयोग्य

incomplete - अपूर्ण

inconvenient - असुविधाजनक

incorrect - असत्य, गलत

independent - स्वाधीन, स्वतन्त्र

indescribable - अनिर्वचनीय

indestructible - अविनाशी

Indian - भारतीय, हिन्दुस्तानी

individual - व्यक्तिगत, निजी

indivisible - अविभाज्य

indoor - घर का, भीतरी

inefficient - अकुशल

infamous - बदनाम

infectious - संक्रामक

inferior - नीचे का, निचला, हीन

influenced - प्रभावित

initiated - दीक्षित

injured - घायल, ज़ख़्मी

innocent - भोला-भाला, निर्दोष

intellectual - बौद्धिक

intelligent - समझदार, बुद्धिमान, अक्लमंद

intense - तीव्र

interesting - दिलचस्प, रुचिकर

international - अन्तर्राष्ट्रीय

intimate - जिगरी, घनिष्ट

invisible - अदृश्य

irritable - चिड़चिड़ा

J

jealous - ईर्ष्यावान

joined - सम्मिलित, युक्त

joyful - आनन्दित, आनन्दमय

just a little - ज़रा सा

K

knowledgeable - ज्ञानवान

known - विदित, सूचित

L

lame - लंगड़ा

large - विशाल, बड़ा, विस्तृत

last - अन्तिम, आख़री

last (previous) - पिछला

late - देर

lazy - आलसी

leading - प्रमुख, प्रधान

lean - दुबला-पतला

learned - विद्वान

least - कम से कम,
सब से छोटा, लघुतम

left (over) - बचा हुआ

left (side) - बायाँ

legal - कानूनी, वैध

lengthwise - लंबाई में

less - कम

light - हल्का

liked - पसन्द

likely - संभावनीय

limited - सीमित

limitless - असीम

little (quantity) - थोड़ा

lively - जीवित, ज़िन्दा,
जीता-जागता

local - स्थानीय, स्थान का

lonely - अकेला

long - लम्बा

loose - ढीला

low - नीचा

loyal - वफ़ादार, नमक हलाल

lucky - भाग्यवान, भाग्यशाली

lumpy - ढेलेदार

M

mad (crazy) - पागल

magical - जादुई

main - प्रमुख

majestic - शानदार, ऐश्वर्यवान्

many - अनेक, बहुत

marine - समुद्री

married - विवाहित, शादीशुदा

masculine - पुलिंग

mature - परिपक्व

mauve - बैंगनी

maximum - अधिकतम,
उच्चतम

medium - माध्यम

melodious - मधुर

mental - मानसिक

mere - केवल, मात्र

merry - प्रफुल्ल, आनंदित

messy - गन्दा

metaphysical - आध्यात्मिक,
अतिसूक्ष्म, अशरीरी

middle - मध्य

mighty - शक्तिशाली, प्रबल

mild - मृदु, कोमल

mild (of person) - शरीफ़

minimal - सूक्ष्मातिसूक्ष्म

minimum - कम से कम

minus - कम कर के, घटा के

mischievous - शरारती, नटखट

miserable - दुःखी

miserly - कंजूस

misty, hazy - धुँधला

mixed - मिश्रित, एकमेक

mixed-up - उलटा-सीधा

modern - आधुनिक

more - और
most - अधिक, सब से अधिक, सब से ज़्यादा
much - काफ़ी, अधिक, बहुत-सा
multi-colored - रंग-विरंग
mysterious - रहस्यमय

N

naked - नंगा
narrow - सँकरा, तंग
narrow (very) - संकीर्ण
national - राष्ट्रीय
natural - स्वाभाविक
naughty - शरारती
nearby - पास का
neat - साफ़
necessary - आवश्यक, ज़रूरी
needy - ज़रूरतमंद
neutral - तटस्थ, निष्पक्ष
new - नया
next - अगला, दूसरा
nice - बढ़िया
no - नहीं
noble - अभिजात, शरीफ
noisy - शोर करने वाला
normal - साधारण
north - उत्तर

O

obliged - आभारी, अनुगृहीत
obstructing - बाधक
obvious - स्पष्ट
oily - तेलिया
okay (O.K.) - ठीक
old - पुराना, (old age) - बूढ़ा
only - केवल, सिर्फ़
orange - नारंगी, संतरा
ordinary - साधारण, आम, मामूली
other - अन्य, और
outer - बाहरी

P

pale - पीला, फीका
parallel - समानान्तर
particular - खास
passionate - कामुक
past - अतीत
peculiar - अजीब, अजीबोगरीब
percent - प्रतिशत
perfect - पूर्ण
permanent - टिकाऊ, स्थायी
perplexed - व्याकुल
personal - व्यक्तिगत, निजी
pervading - सर्वव्याप्त, व्यापक
physical - भौतिक, स्थूल, शारीरिक
pieces (small) - टुकड़े टुकड़े

pink - गुलाबी

pleased - खुश, प्रसन्न

pleasing - दिलपसन्द

plus - जमा

pointless - बेकार

polite - शिष्ट, नम्र, विनम्र

poor - गरीब, दरिद्र, निर्धन

poor (wretched) - बेकार

popular - लोकप्रिय

positive - निश्चित, पक्का

possible - संभव

powerful - शक्तिशाली, प्रबल

powerless - शक्तिहीन

practical - व्यवहारिक

precious - मूल्यवान, बहुमूल्य

pregnant - गर्भवती

prepared - तत्पर, तैयार

present - मौजूद, उपस्थित

pretty - सुन्दर

previous - पूर्व, पहला, पिछला

primary - प्रमुख, प्रथम

prime - प्रधान

private - गुप्त, अकेले में, एकान्त में

profitable - लाभदायक

profound - गहरा, गंभीर, गहन

prohibited - वर्जित

proper - उचित

prosperous - धनवान, समृद्ध

proud - अभिमानी

psychological - मानसिक

public - आम, सर्वजनिक

puffy - फूला हुआ

pure - निर्मल, शुद्ध

purple - बैंगनी, जामुनी

Q

queer - अजीब, विचित्र

quick - तेज़, जल्दी

quiet (peaceful) - शान्त

quite, quite a few - काफ़ी

R

racial - जाति का

rapt - विभोर

rare - अनोखा, अनूठा

raw (unripe) - कच्चा

ready - तैयार

real (true) - सही, सच्चा, वास्तविक, असली

reassured - आश्वस्त

red - लाल

regional - प्रदेशीय

relevant - संबंधित

reliable - विश्वसनीय

religious - धार्मिक

remainder (rest of) - बाकी, शेष

respected - प्रतिष्ठित आदरणीय, मान्य

respectful - सादर

responsible - उत्तरदायी

restless - बेचैन

revered - पूज्य, माननीय

reverse - उलटा, विपरीत

rich - अमीर, धनी

right (direction) - दाहिना

right (exact) - ठीक, सही, उचित

ripe - पक्का, पक्व, तैयार

rotten - ख़राब

rough - कठोर

rough (skin) - खुरखुरा

round - गोल

royal - राजकीय

rude - उद्धत, अशिष्ट

ruined - बर्बाद

S

sad - दुःखी, उदास

safe - सुरक्षित, रक्षित

salty - नमकीन

same - ऐसा, बराबर, समान

satisfactory - संतोषजनक

secluded - एकांत

second - दूसरा

secret - गुप्त

selfish - स्वार्थी

senior - वरिष्ठ, ज्येष्ठ

sensitive - संवेदनशील

sentient - चेतन

sentimental - भावुक

separate - अलग

serious - गंभीर

several - कई

severe - सख्त, कठोर

sharp - तेज़, पैना

sharp (mind, intellect) - तेज़, तीव्र

shattered - नाश

shiny - जगमग

short - छोटा

shut - बन्द

shy - शर्मीला, शर्मिन्दा

sick - बीमार

significant - अर्थवान, सार्थक

silent - मौन

simple - सरल

sincere - निष्कपट, सच्चा

sinful - पापमय

single - अकेला, एकमात्र

skilled - कुशल

slippery - चिकना

slow - धीरे, आहिस्ता

small - छोटा, तनिक

smart - समझदार

smooth - चिकना, बराबर

sociable - मिलनसार

soft - नरम, कोमल, मुलायम

solidified - घनीभूत

some - कुछ

sour - खट्टा	sure - निश्चित, पक्का
south - दक्षिण	suspended - लंबित
special - विशेष, खास	sweet - मीठा, मधुर
spiritual - आत्मिक, आध्यात्मिक	symbolic - प्रतीकात्मक

T

splendid - शानदार, भव्य	talkative - बातूनी
spoiled - ख़राब	tame (domesticated) - पालतू
square (level) - चौरस	tangled - उलझा हुआ
stable - अचल, स्थिर	tasteless - फीका
stale - बासी	temporary - क्षणिक
stingy - कंजूस, कृपण	terrible - भयंकर
stormy - तूफ़ानी	thick - मोटा, घोर
straight - सीधा	thin - पतला, बारीक
strange - अजीब, अनोखा, विचित्र	thousands - हज़ारों
strict - कड़ा	tight - तंग, कसा हुआ
strong - बलवान, मज़बूत, प्रबल	tiny - बहुत छोटा, नन्हा
stubborn - हठी, जिद्दी	tired - थका
stuffy (head) - भारीपन	tolerant - सहनशील
stupid, foolish - मूर्ख, बेवकूफ़	too much - बहुत अधिक
subtle - सूक्ष्म	total - सम्पूर्ण, सकल, पूरा, सारा
successful - सफल	tough - कड़ा, मज़बूत
such - ऐसा, इस प्रकार का, इस तरह का	tragic - दुःखांत
	tranquil - शान्त
such a kind - ऐसा	transient - अस्थिर, अनित्य, क्षणिक
sudden - अचानक	
suitable - उपयुक्त, उचित, ठीक	transitory - क्षणिक
superior - उच्चतर	tricky - चालाक
supreme - परम	triumphant - विजयी
	troubled - परेशान

true - सत्य, सच्चा, यथार्थ
trustwowrthy - विश्वसनीय
truthful - सत्यशील
twin - जुड़वाँ

U

ugly - कुरूप, भद्दा
unanimous - एक मत
unaware - अचेत, अनजान
uncertain - अनिश्चित, संदिग्ध
uncommon - अनूठा
unconditional - बिना शर्त
unconscious - बेहोश
understood - विदित
undivided - अभिन्न
uneasy - व्याकुल
uneducated - अनपढ़,
    बिना पढ़ा लिखा,
unemployed - निठल्ला,
    बेरोज़गार
unequal - असमान
uneven - असम
unexpected - इत्तफ़ाक़ी
unfair - अनुचित
unfit - अयोग्य
unfortunate - अभाग्य
ungrateful - अकृतज्ञ
unhappy - दुःखी, अप्रसन्न
unique - अनुपम, विलक्षण
unkind - निर्दय

unlikely - असम्भव
unlimited - असीम
unlucky - दुर्भाग्यशाली, मनहूस
unnatural - अस्वाभाविक
unnecessary - अनावश्यक
unripe - अपरिपक्व
unripe - कच्चा
unsafe - ख़तरनाक
unstable - अस्थिर, चंल
unsuitable - अयोग्य
untimely - बेवक्त
unusual (peculiar) - विचित्र
upcoming - आने-वाला
upright - खड़ा
upside-down - उलटा-पुलटा
useful - हितकर, लाभदायक,
    उपयोगी, उपयुक्त
useless - बेकार, फ़ालतू
usual - सामान्य, साधारण

V

vacant - शून्य, खाली
vain - प्रमादी
valid - ठोस
valuable - मूल्यवान
various - विभिन्न, भाँति-भाँति
vast - विशाल, विस्तृत
vegetarian - शाकाहारी
venerable - आदरणीय
vertical - खड़ा, लम्बवत्

very - बहुत
vibrant - स्पन्दमान, कंपमान
victorious - विजयी
violent - हिंसक
virtuous - गुणवान, गुणवंत
visible - दृश्यमान
void - शून्य
voluntary - ऐच्छिक

W

warm - गरम
wasted - बर्बाद
wavy - लहरदार
weak - कमज़ोर, दुर्बल
wealthy - अमीर, धनवान
weary - निढाल
west - पश्चिम
wet - गीला
white - सफेद
whole - पूरा, सम्पूर्ण, समस्त
wicked - पापमय
wide - चौड़ा
wild - जंगली
wise - विद्वान, समझदार
wonderful - अद्भुत
worse - बदतर, और बुरा
worst - सब से बुरा
worthless - निकम्मा
worthy - योग्य
wounded - घायल

wrecked - ख़राब
wretched - बेकार
wrong - गलत

Y

yellow - पीला
young - युवा

Nouns

Nouns are either masculine or feminine, and the gender of each noun listed in this chapter is indicated by (m) for masculine or (f) for feminine. When learning a noun, it is essential to learn its gender, because adjectives, and verbs in certain constructions, agree with the gender of the noun. Nouns are listed in their singular form. If a noun is plural or followed by a postposition (hence, must be put in the oblique case), the following rules apply:

Plural Formation of Nouns
Direct Case

Recall that a noun in the direct case is one not followed by a postposition.

Masculine Nouns

Only masculine nouns that end in आ (e.g., लड़का 'boy') change in spelling to show the plural. The आ ending of these nouns becomes ए in the plural:

एक लड़का   one boy (sing.)   दो लड़के   two boys (pl.)

All other masculine nouns do not undergo any modification in the plural:

एक आदमी   one man   दो आदमी   two men
एक सेब   one apple   बहुत सेब   many apples

Note: Adjectives will still agree with the plural number of a noun whether or not the noun shows the plural ending. (Sometimes this is the only indication that a noun is plural.)

अच्छे सेब   good apples

49

Feminine Nouns

All feminine nouns show the plural by adding either याँ or एँ to their endings as follows:

याँ Ending

The following add याँ to form the plural:

nouns ending in इ – जाति (caste) जातियाँ (castes)
nouns ending in ई – लड़की (girl) लड़कियाँ (girls)[1]
nouns ending in या – चिड़िया (bird) चिड़ियाँ (birds)

एँ Ending

The following add एँ to form the plural:

nouns ending in आ – भाषा (language) भाषाएँ (languages)
nouns ending in अ – किताब (book) किताबें (books)
nouns ending in उ – वस्तु (thing) वस्तुएँ (things)
nouns ending in ऊ – बहू (daughter-in-law)

बहुएँ (daughters-in-law)[2]

IMPORTANT NOTE:

There are no articles such as 'a' or 'the' in Hindi; these are understood to be included in the noun. The word एक 'one' can be used for the English article 'a'.

---

[1] Note: ई is 'replaced' by इ
[2] Note: ऊ is 'replaced' by उ

Nouns in the Oblique Case

If a noun is followed by a postposition (e.g., में 'in,' को 'to,' पर 'on') then it must be put in the oblique case.

Masculine nouns ending in आ have ए endings in the oblique singular and ओं endings in the oblique plural:

लड़का — boy (direct case)
लड़के को — to the boy (oblique singular)
लड़कों को — to the boys (oblique plural)

Masculine nouns that do not end in आ change their ending only in the oblique plural:

दिन — day (direct case)
दिन में — in a day (oblique singular)
दिनों में — in days (oblique plural)

Similarly, feminine nouns are modified only in the oblique plural:

किताब — book (direct case)
किताब में — in the book (oblique singular)
किताबों में — in the books (oblique plural)

Grammatical Cases of
Masculine and Feminine Nouns

	Direct		Oblique	
	SINGULAR	PLURAL	SINGULAR	PLURAL
room	कमरा (m)	कमरे	कमरे	कमरों
day	दिन (m)	दिन	दिन	दिनों
man	आदमी (m)	आदमी	आदमी	आदमिओं
caste	जाति (f)	जातियाँ	जाति	जातियों
girl	लड़की (f)	लड़कियाँ	लड़की	लड़कियों
bird	चिड़िया (f)	चिड़ियाँ	चिड़िया	चिड़ियों
thing	वस्तु (f)	वस्तुएँ	वस्तु	वस्तुओं
language	भाषा (f)	भाषाएँ	भाषा	भाषाओं
book	किताब (f)	किताबें	किताब	किताबों

Masculine examples:

This is the right room. यह ठीक कमरा है। (direct sing.)

These rooms are good. ये कमरे अच्छे हैं। (direct pl.)

The book is in the room. किताब कमरे में है। (oblique sing.)

There are men in the rooms. कमरों में आदमी हैं। (oblique pl.)

Feminine examples:

This is a good book. यह अच्छी किताब है। (direct sing.)

These books are not good. ये किताबें अच्छी नहीं हैं। (direct pl.)

The apple is on the book. सेब किताब पर है। (oblique sing.)

The bird is on the books. चिड़िया किताबों पर है। (oblique pl.)

A

abuse - (f) गाली

acceptance - (f) स्वीकृति

accident - (f) दुर्घटना

account - (m) हिसाब

acidity - (m) खट्टापन

acquaintance - (f) जानकारी,
    जान-पहचान

address - (m) पता

adjective - (m) विशेषण

adult - (m) वयस्क

advantage - (m) लाभ, फ़ायदा

adverb - (m) क्रिया-विशेषण

advertisement - (m) विज्ञापन

advice - (m) उपदेश, (f) सलाह,
    नसीहत

afternoon - (m) दोपहर, मध्यांह

age - (f) उम्र, आयु

air - (f) हवा, (m) वायु

airplane - (m) हवाई जहाज़

alcohol - (f) शराब

alertness - (f) सजगता

alley - (f) गली

alligator - (m) घड़ियाल

almond - (m) बादाम

ambassador - (m) राजदूत

animal - (m) पशु, जानवर

anise - (f) सौंफ

answer - (m) उत्तर, जवाब

ant (black) - (m) मकोड़ा, चींटा

ant (red) - (f) मकोड़ी, चींटी

anxiety - (f) चिन्ता, फ़िक्र

apology - (f) क्षमा, माफ़ी

apparatus - (m) उपकरण

appearance - (f) उपस्थिति, सूरत

apple - (m) सेब

appreciation - (f) प्रशंसा, प्रशस्ति

approval - (m) स्वीकृति, मन्ज़ूरी

apricot - (f) खुर्मानी

area - (m) इलाक़ा

argument - (f) बहस, (m) झगड़ा,
    वाद-विवाद

arm - (m) बाहु, बाज़ू, भुज

armpit - (f) बगल

army - (f) सेना

arrangement - (m) प्रबन्ध

arrest - (f) गिरफ़्तारी

arrogance - (f) गुस्ताख़ी, (m)
    अक्खड़पन

art - (f) कला

article (written) - (m) अनुच्छेद

artist - (m) कलाकार, चित्रकार

ashram - (m) आश्रम

aspect - (m) पक्ष

aspirant - (m) साधक

assistant - (m) सहायक

assurance - (m) पक्की बात,
    निश्चय

astrologer - (m) ज्योतिषी

astrology - (m) ज्योतिष

atmosphere - (m) वातावरण, वायुमण्डल

atom - (m) अणु

attachment - (m) मोह (f) लगन

attack - (m) आक्रमण

attention - (m) ध्यान

attraction - (m) आकर्षण

audience - (m) श्रोता, दर्शक

author - (m) कर्ता, लेखक

authority - (m) अधिकार

autumn - (m) पतझड़, (f) शरद

awareness - (m) साधना, (f) अवगति, चेतना

B

back - (f) पीठ

backbiter - (m) चुगलख़ोर

backbiting - (f) चुगली

bacteria - (m) जीवाणु

bag - (m) थैला

balance (scale) - (m) तराज़ू, सन्तुलन

ball - (f) गेंद, (m) गोला

balloon - (m) गुब्बारा

bamboo - (m) बाँस

ban - (m) निषेध

banana - (m) केला

bandage - (f) पट्टी

bandit - (m) डाकू

bangle - (f) चूड़ी

bank (river) - (m) किनारा

barbarian - (m) बर्बर

barrier - (m) आड़

basil - (m) तुलसी

basis - (m) आधार

basket - (f) टोकरी

bath- (m) स्नान

bathroom - (m) गुस्ल-खाना, स्नान घर

bazaar - (m) बाज़ार

beach - (m) समुद्र-तट

beak - (f) चोंच

beam (wood) - (f) कड़ी

bear - (m) भालू

beard - (f) दाढ़ी

beauty - (f) सुन्दरता, (m) सौन्दर्य

bed - (m) बिस्तर, पलंग

bed (flower ~) - (f) क्यारी

bedcover - (f) चादर

bedcover - (m) पलंग-पोश

bedding - (m) बिस्तरा

bee - (f) मधुमक्खी, भँवरा

beet - (m) चुकन्दर

beggar - (m) भिखारी

beginning - (m) आरंभ, शुरू, शुरुआत

being (state of) - (m) अस्तित्व

belief - (m) विश्वास

bell - (f) घंटी

belt - (f) पेटी

benefit - (m) लाभ, फ़ायदा

bird - (f) चिड़िया, पक्षी

birth - (m) जन्म

birthday - (m) जन्म दिन

blanket - (m) कम्बल

blessing - (m) आशीर्वाद

bliss - (m) आनन्द

blood - (m) खून, रक्त, लहू, रुधिर

board - (m) तख्ता

boat - (f) नाव

body - (m) देह, शरीर, तन

boldness - (f) दिलेरी, (m) साहस

bone - (f) हड्डी

book - (f) पुस्तक, किताब

border - (m) छोर

bottom - (m) तल

boundary - (f) सीमा, हद, (m) घेरा

bowl - (m) कटोरा, (f) कटोरी

box - (m) डिब्बा, संदूक

boy - (m) लड़का

brain - (m) दिमाग, मस्तिष्क

branch - (f) शाखा

brass - (m) पीतल

bread - (f) रोटी

bread (loaf) - (f) डबल रोटी

breakfast - (m) नाश्ता

breast - (m) स्तन

breath - (m) श्वास, (f) साँस

brick - (f) ईंट

bride - (f) दुलहन

bridge - (m) पुल

brilliance - (m) नूर

broom - (m) झाड़ू

brother - (m) भाई, बंधु, भ्राता

bucket - (f) बाल्टी

bud - (f) कली

buffalo - (f) भैंस

building - (f) इमारत

bull - (m) साँड़

bullock - (m) बैल

bully - (m) गुंडा

bumblebee - (m) भ्रमर

bunch - (m) गुच्छा

bundle - (f) गठरी, पोटली

bush - (f) झाड़ी

business - (m) व्यापार, व्यवसाय

butter - (m) मक्खन

butter (clarified) - (m) घी

butterfly - (f) तितली

buttocks - (m) चूतड़

C

cabbage - (f) बन्द गोभी

cafe - (m) ढाबा

cage - (m) पिंजरा

calculation - (m) हिसाब, (f) गिनती	chain - (f) कड़ी
calf - (m) बछड़ा	chair - (f) कुर्सी
camel - (m) ऊँट	challenge - (m) मुकाबला
candle - (f) मोमबत्ती	chameleon - (m) गिरगिट
canvas - (m) पटल	chance - (m) भाग्य, संयोग
cap - (f) टोपी	channel - (f) नाली, (m) नाला
capability - (f) क्षमता	chapaatee - (f) चपाती
capital (city) - (f) राजधानी	charm - (m) लावण्य
capture - (f) गिरफ़्त	cheek - (m) गाल
car - (f) गाड़ी	cheese - (m) पनीर
caravan - (m) काफ़िला	cheetah - (m) चीता
cardamom - (f) इलायची	charity - (f) कृपा, दान,
care - (f) देखभाल, सावधानी	दयालुता
carelessness - (f) लापरवाही	chess - (m) शतरंज
carpet - (m) कालीन	chest - (f) छाती, (m) सीना
carrot - (f) गाजर	chick - (m) मुर्गी का बच्चा
case (affair, matter) - (m) मामला	chick pea - (m) चना
caste - (f) जाति	chicken - (f) मुर्गी, (m) चूज़ा
cat - (f) बिल्ली	chief - (m) मुख्य
catastrophe - (f) मुसीबत	child - (m) बच्चा, बालक
cauliflower - (f) फूल गोभी	childhood - (m) बचपन
cause - (m) कारण, हेतु	chilli - (f) मिर्च
caution - (f) सावधानी	chin - (f) ठुड्डी
cave - (f) गुफा	choice – (f) पसन्द
celebration - (m) समारोह	cinnamon - (f) दालचीनी
center - (m) केन्द्र	circle - (m) गोला
centipede - (f) गोजर	circumstance - (f) परिस्थिति
century - (f) सदी, शताब्दी	city - (m) नगर, शहर
certainty - (m) यकीन	class (social) - (m) वर्ग

clay - (f) मिट्टी

clay pot - (m) घड़ा

clock - (f) घड़ी

cloth - (m) कपड़ा, वस्त्र

clothing - (m.pl.) कपड़े

cloud - (m) बादल, मेघ

cloves - (m) लौंग

clue - (m) पता

coal - (m) कोयला

coast - (m) तट

coconut - (m) नारियल

coincidence - (m) इत्तफ़ाक़

cold (sickness) - (m) जुकाम

colony - (f) बस्ती

color - (m) रंग

comb - (f) कंघी, (m) कंघा

combination - (m) संयोजन

comfort - (m) आराम

commotion - (f) खलबली

communication - (m) संचार, संचारण

companion - (m) साथी

company - (m) संग

compassion - (f) करुणा

competence - (f) क्षमता, योग्यता

complaint - (f) शिकायत

complication - (f) उलझन, (m) उलझाव

conceit - (m) घमंड

concept - (f) धारणा, मान्यता

concern - (m) संबंध, (f) फ़िक्र

conclusion - (m) निष्कर्ष, नतीजा

condition - (m) हाल, (f) शर्त, वस्था

confession - (m) इकरार

confidence - (m) आत्म विश्वास

confluence - (m) संगम

confrontation - (m) मुकाबला

confusion - (m) गड़बड़

congratulations - (f) बधाई, मुबारकी

consciousness - (f) चेतना

consonant (letter) - (m) अक्षर

constipation - (m) कब्ज़

construction - (m) निर्माण

contact - (m) सम्पर्क

container - (m) डिब्बा

context - (m) प्रसंग

continent - (m) महाद्वीप

contribution - (m) योगदान

control - (m) निरोध, नियंत्रण

conversation - (f) बात-चीत

cooperation - (m) सहयोग

coriander - (m) धनिया

cord - (m) सूत, सूत्र

corn - (f) मक्की

corner - (m) कोना

correspondence - (m) पत्र-व्यवहार

correspondent - (m) संवाददाता

cost - (f) कीमत

cough - (f) खाँसी

country - (m) देश

country (foreign) - (m) विदेश

couple - (m) जोड़ा, (f) जोड़ी

courage - (m) साहस, (f) हिम्मत

courtesy - (f) तमीज़, (m) शिष्टाचार

cover - (m) ढक्कन, आवरण

cow - (f) गाय

coward - (m) भीरु, डरपोक, कायर

cowardice - (f) भीरुता, कायरता

cradle - (m) झूला

cream - (f) मलाई

creator - (m) रचयिता

credit - (m) उधार

creeper - (f) बेल

crime - (m) अपराध, जुर्म

criminal - (m) मुजरिम

criticism - (f) आलोचना

crocodile - (m) मगरमच्छ

crow - (m) कौआ

crowd - (f) भीड़

crown - (m) मुकुट, ताज

cry - (f) चिल्लाहट

cucumber - (m) खीरा

cumin - (m) जीरा

cup - (m) प्याला

cupboard - (f) अलमारी

cure - (m) इलाज

curiosity - (f) जिज्ञासा

curse - (m) शाप, श्राप

cushion - (m) गद्दा

custom - (m) रिवाज

customer - (m) खरीदार

D

damage - (m) नुक्सान, (f) हानि

dampness - (f) सीलन

darkness - (m) अँधेरा

date - (f) तारीख

daughter - (f) बेटी

dawn - (m) उदय, प्रभात, सूर्य का उदय

day - (m) दिन, दिवस

death - (f) मृत्यु, (m) देहान्त

debate - (m) संवाद

debt - (m) ऋण

decade - (m) दशक

decision - (m) निर्णय

declaration – (m) एलान

deer - (m) मृग, हिरन

defeat - (f) हार

defect - (f) बुराई, त्रुटि, (m) दोष

degree - (f) उपाधि

deity - (m) देवता, (f) देवी

demand - (f) माँग

departure - (f) बिदा

depth - (f) गहराई

description - (m) वर्णन

desert - (m) रेगिस्तान

desire - (f) अभिलाषा, इच्छा

destiny - (m) भाग्य

destruction - (m) विनाश

detail - (m) विवरण, ब्योरा

development - (f) उन्नति

devil - (m) शैतान

dialogue - (m) संवाद

diamond - (m) हीरा

diarrhea - (m) दस्त, (f) पेचिश

dictionary - (m) शब्दकोश

diet - (m) आहार

difference - (m) अंतर, (f) भिन्नता

difficulty - (f) मुश्किल, तकलीफ़

digestion - (m) पाचनशक्ति, हाजमा

dignity - (m) गौरव, इक़बाल

direction - (f) तरफ़, दिशा

dirt - (f) मिट्टी, गन्दगी

disappointment - (f) निराशा

disaster - (f) तबाही, आपत्

disciple - (m) शिष्य, चेला

discipline - (m) अनुशासन

discount - (f) रिआयत, छूट

discovery - (m) आविष्कार, (f) खोज

discrimination - (m) विवेक

discussion - (m) वाद-विवाद, (f) चर्चा

disease - (m) रोग

disgrace - (m) अपमान, (f) बेइज़्ज़ती

dishes - (m) बर्तन

dishonesty - (f) बेईमानी

dishonor - (m) अपमान

disinterest - (f) अरुचि, (m) उपेक्षा

display - (m) प्रदर्शन, (f) दिखाई

distance - (f) दूरी

district - (m) जिला

divinity - (m) देवत्व

divorce - (m) तलाक

dizziness - (m) सिर का चक्कर

dog - (m) कुत्ता

donkey - (m) गधा

door - (m) दरवाज़ा, द्वार

dot - (m) बिन्दु

doubt - (f) शंका, सन्देह, (m) शक

dough - (m) गुँधा हुआ आटा

dozen - (m) दर्जन

drawer - (f) दराज़

drop - (f) बूँद

drunk - (m) शराबी

duality - (m) द्वैत

duck - (f) बत्तख

duration - (m) दौरान, (f) अवधि

dust - (m) धूल

duty - (m) कर्तव्य, धर्म, फ़र्ज़,

duty (religious) - (m) फ़र्ज़, धर्म

dysentery - (m) दस्त

E

eagerness - (f) उत्सुकता

eagle - (m) गरुड़, बाज़

ear - (m) कान

earth - (f) पृथ्वी, ज़मीन

ease - (f) राहत

east - (m) पूर्व, पूरब

echo - (f) प्रतिध्वनि

eclipse - (m) ग्रहण

economics - (m) अर्थशास्त्र

economy - (m) अर्थव्यवस्था।

edge - (m) धार

education - (f) शिक्षा

effect (influence) - (m) असर, प्रभाव

efficiency - (m) कुशलता

effort - (m) प्रयत्न, प्रयास, यत्न, (f) कोशिश

egg - (m) अंडा

eggplant - (m) बैंगन

elbow - (f) कोहनी

elders - (m.pl.) बड़े-बूढ़े, (m) बुज़ुर्ग

election - (m) चुनाव

electrician - (m) बिजली वाला

electricity - (f) बिजली

element - (m) तत्त्व

elephant - (f) हाथी

embassy - (m) राज आवास

emergency - (m) संकट

emotion - (f) भावना

end - (m) अंत, आखिर

enemy - (m) शत्रु

energy - (f) शक्ति, ऊर्जा

English - (f) अँग्रेज़ी

enquiry - (f) पूछ-ताछ

entanglement - (f) उलझन

entertainment - (m) मनोरंजन

entrance - (m) प्रवेश

entrance (path, route) - (m) मार्ग, पथ

envelope - (m) लिफ़ाफ़ा

envy - (f) ईर्ष्या

episode - (f) उपकथा

equipment - (m) सामान, उपकरण

era - (m) युग

essay - (m) निबन्ध

establishment - (m) संस्थापन, संस्थान

eternity - (f) नित्यता, शाश्वतता

etiquette - (m) शिष्टाचार

evening - (f) शाम, संध्या, सांझ

event - (f) घटना

evil - (f) बला

evolution - (m) विकास

exaggeration - (f) अतिशयोक्ति

example - (m) उदाहरण

excellence - (m) श्रेष्ठता

exchange - (m) आदान-प्रदान

excitement - (f) उत्तेजना,
(m) जोश

excrement - (f) टट्टियाँ, (m) मल

excuse - (m) बहाना, (f) क्षमा,
माफ़ी

exhaustion - (f) थकान

existence - (f) सत्ता

expectation - (f) आशा, उम्मीद,
अपेक्षा

expenditure - (m) खर्च, व्यय

experience - (m) अनुभव,
(f) अनुभूति

experiment - (m) परीक्षण

exploration - (m) छान-बीन,
अनुसंधान

explosion - (m) विस्फोट,
धमाका

expression - (m) कथन,
(f) अभिव्यक्ति

extent - (f) हद

extra - (m) अतिरिक्त, फ़ालतू

extremity - (m) छोर

eye - (f) आँख, नयन, नेत्र

eyelid - (f) पलक

F

face - (m) चेहरा

fact - (m) तथ्य

failure - (f) असफलता

faint - (f) मूर्च्छा, बेहोशी

fairness - (f) ईमानदारी

fairy - (f) अप्सरा

fame - (m) यश, (f) कीर्ति

family - (m) परिवार, कुटुम्ब

famine - (m) अकाल

fan - (m) पंखा

farewell - (f) विदाई

farmer - (m) किसान

fate - (m) भाग्य, प्रारब्ध,
(f) नियति, किस्मत

father - (m) पिता, बाप

fatigue - (f) थकान

fault - (m) दोष

favor - (m) उपकार

fear - (m) भय, डर

feast - (m) भोज, उत्सव

feat - (m) कमाल

feeling - (f) भावना, अनुभूति

fence - (f) बाड़

fenugreek - (f) मेथी

festival - (m) उत्सव, त्योहार

fever - (m) बुखार

field - (m) खेत

fight - (f) लड़ाई

finger - (f) उँगली, अँगुली	fork - (m) काँटा
fingernail - (m) नाखून	form - (m) रूप
fire - (f) आग, अग्नि	fortune - (f) किस्मत, भाग्य
fish - (f) मछली	fountain - (m) झरना
fist - (m) मुट्ठी	fox - (f) लोमड़ी
flame - (f) ज्वाला, लपट	fragrance - (f) खुशबू
flattery - (f) चापलूसी, चुपड़ी बात	fraud (deceit) - (m) धोखा, छल
flaw - (f) बुराई	freedom - (f) मुक्ति, स्वतंत्रता
flea - (m) पिस्सू	French - (m) फ़्रांसीसी
flesh - (m) माँस, गोश्त	friend - (m) दोस्त, मित्र, यार (f) सहेली
flight - (m) उड़ान	friendship - (m) मित्रता, दोस्ती
flood - (m) बाढ़	frog - (m) मेढक
floor - (m) फ़र्श	fruit - (m) फल
floor (storey) - (f) मंजिल	frustration - (f) बेबसी
flour - (m) आटा	fun - (m) मज़ा
flower - (m) फूल, पुष्प	future - (f) भविष्य
fly - (f) मक्खी	
fog - (m) कोहरा, कुहरा, (f) धुंध	**G**
fondness - (m) शौक	gain - (m) लाभ
food - (m) खाना, भोजन	gamble - (m) जुआ
fool - (m) बुद्धू	game - (m) खेल
foot - (m) पैर, पाँव, पद	gangster - (m) गुंडा
footprint - (m) पदचिन्ह	gap (split) - (f) दरार, (m) फासला
force - (m) बल, (f) ज़ोर	garbage - (m) कूड़ा
forehead - (m) माथा, ललाट, मस्तक	garden - (m) बाग, बगीचा, (f) बगिया
foreigner - (m) विदेशी	gardener - (m) माली
forest - (m) वन, जंगल	garland - (f) माला
forgiveness - (f) माफ़ी, क्षमा	gem - (f) मणि

62

general (army) - (m) सेनापति
generation - (f) पीढ़ी
generosity - (f) उदारता
gentleman - (m) सज्जन
ghost - (m) भूत
gift - (m) उपहार, (f) भेंट
gift (to Guru) - (f) गुरु दक्षिणा
ginger - (m) अदरक
girl - (f) लड़की, कन्या
gland - (f) गिलटी
glass - (m) प्याला, गिलास
glass pane - (m) शीशा
glasses - (f) ऐनक, (m) चश्मा
glimpse - (f) झाँकी, झलक
glory - (m) महिमा, यश
glue - (f) गोंद
goal - (m) लक्ष्य
goat - (f) बकरी
gold - (m) सोना, स्वर्ण
good fortune - (m) सौभाग्य
good wishes - (f.pl.) शुभकामनाएँ
goodness - (f) अच्छाई, भलाई
goods - (m) माल, सामान
gossip - (f) गप-शप
government - (f) सरकार
grace - (f) शोभा, कृपा
grain - (m) दाना, अनाज
grammar - (m) व्याकरण
grape - (m) अंगूर

grass - (m) घास
grass blade - (m) तिनका
gratefulness - (m) आभार
gratitude - (m) कृतज्ञता
grave - (m) कब्र
gravel - (f) बजरी
gravity - (m) गुरुत्वाकर्षण
greatness - (f) महानता
green lentil - (m) मूँग
green pepper - (f) शिमला मिर्च
greenery - (f) हरियाली
grief - (m) दुःख, शोक
groom - (m) दुल्हा
ground - (m) ज़मीन
group - (m) समूह, समुदाय
growl - (m) गुर्राहट
grunt - (f) घुरघुर
guard - (m) पहरा, संतरी
guess - (m) अनुमान, अन्दाज़ा
guest - (m) मेहमान, (f) अतिथि
guide - (m) मार्गदर्शक
gums - (m) मसूड़ा
gun - (m) बन्दूक
guru - (m) गुरु
gust - (m) झकोरा, हवा का झोंका
gutter (sewer) - (m) नाला

H

habit - (f) आदत
hail - (m) ओला

hair - (m.pl.) बाल

hammer - (f) हथौड़ा

hand - (m) हाथ

handkerchief - (m) रूमाल

happiness - (m) सुख, (f) खुशी

harm - (m) हानि, नुक्सान

hat - (f) टोपी

hate - (f) घृणा

hawk - (m) बाज़

head - (m) सिर

headache - (m) सिर-दर्द

health - (m) स्वास्थ्य,
   (f) तंदुरुस्ती, तबियत

heart - (m) दिल, हृदय

heat - (f) गर्मी, (m) ताप

heaven - (m) स्वर्ग

heel - (f) एड़ी

height - (f) ऊँचाई

heir - (f) उत्तराधिकारी

hell - (m) नरक

hermitage - (m) आश्रम

hero - (m) वीर, शूरवीर

hesitation - (m) संकोच,
   (f) झिझक

Hindi - (f) हिन्दी

hindrance - (m) बाधा, रुकावट

hint - (m) संकेत

hip - (m) कूल्हा

history - (m) इतिहास

hole - (m) छेद

holiday - (f) छुट्टी

holy man - (m) साधु

home - (m) घर, गृह

homework - (m) घर का काम

honesty - (f) ईमानदारी

honey - (m) शहद, मधु

honor - (f) इज़्ज़त, (m) मान

hoof - (m) खुर

hope - (f) आशा, उम्मीद

horn - (m) सींग

horse - (m) घोड़ा, अश्व

hospitality - (m) अतिथि-सत्कार

host - (m) मेहमानदार, मेज़बान

hour - (m) घंटा

house - (m) मकान, घर

human being - (m) इन्सान,
   मनुष्य, मानव

humanity - (m) मानव-जाति,
   मनुष्य-जाति

hunger - (f) भूख

hunter - (m) शिकारी

hurt - (f) चोट

husband - (m) पति

I

ice - (f) बर्फ़

idea - (m) विचार, (f) भावना

image - (m) प्रतिमा, मूर्ति

imagination - (f) कल्पना

imbalance - (m) असन्तुलन

immortality - (f) अमरता

imperfection - (m) अपूर्णता

importance - (m) महत्त्व

impossibility - (m) असंभवता, असंभव बात

impression - (m) छाप, संस्कार

improvement - (f) उन्नति, (m) सुधार

inability - (m) अयोग्यता

inauguration - (m) उद्घाटन

incense - (f) अगरबत्ती

inclination (tilt) - (m) झुकाव

independence - (f) स्वतंत्रता, स्वाधीनता, आज़ादी

India - (m) भारत

Indian - (m.pl.) हिन्दुस्तानी, भारतीय

indication - (m) इशारा

indication, sign - (m) चिन्ह

indifference - (m) उपेक्षा, (f) उदासीनता

indigestion - (m) अपच, (f) बदहज़मी

individual - (m) व्यक्ति

individuality - (m) व्यक्तित्व

infection - (m) संक्रमण

influence - (m) प्रभाव

information - (m) सूचना, (f) ख़बर

inhabitant - (m) निवासी

inheritance - (f) विरासत

injury - (f) चोट

innocence - (m) भोलापन

inquiry - (m) पूछ-ताछ

insanity - (m) पागलपन

insect - (m) कीड़ा

insight (striking idea) - (f) सूझ

insistence - (m) आग्रह

inspection -(m) निरीक्षण

inspiration - (f) प्रेरणा

instant - (m) क्षण

instinct - (m) मूल प्रवृत्ति

institute - (m) संस्थान

instrument - (m) यन्त्र

insurance - (m) बीमा

intellect - (f) बुद्धि, प्रज्ञा

intellectual - (m) प्रबुद्ध व्यक्ति

intelligence - (f) प्रज्ञता, अक्ल

intention - (m) इरादा, अभिप्राय

interest - (f) रुचि, दिलचस्पी

interference - (m) हस्तक्षेप

interruption - (f) रुकावट

intestine - (f) आँत

intoxication - (f) मस्ती, (m) नशा

introduction - (m) परिचय, भूमिका, (f) प्रस्ताव

invasion - (m) आक्रमण

invention - (m) आविष्कार, ईजाद

investigation - (f) छान-बीन, पूछ-ताछ

invitation - (m) निमन्त्रण, न्योता

involvement - (m) उलझाव

iron - (m) लोहा

island - (m) द्वीप

itch - (f) खुजली

J

jackal - (m) सियार

jail - (m) कैदखाना, बन्दीगृह

jar - (f) शीशी

jasmine - (f) चमेली

jaw - (m) जबड़ा

jealousy - (f) ईर्ष्या

jewel - (m) रत्न, (f) मणि

jewelry - (m.pl.) गहने

job - (f) नौकरी

joint - (m) जोड़

joke - (m) मज़ाक, चुटकुला

journey - (f) यात्रा, (m) सफ़र

joy - (m) आनन्द, (f) मौज

judge - (m) न्यायाधीश

jug - (m) जग

juice - (f) रस

junction - (m) संगम

justice - (m) न्याय, इन्साफ़

K

kettle - (f) केतली

key - (f) चाबी

kidnapping - (m) अपहरण

kidney - (m) गुर्दा

kidney bean - (m) राजमाश

kind - (m) प्रकार

kindness - (f) दयालुता, मेहरबानी, नवाज़ी

king - (m) राजा

kingdom - (m) राज्य

kiss - (m) चुंबन

kitchen - (f) रसोई

kite - (m) पतंग

knee - (m) घुटना

knife - (m) चाकू

knot - (f) गाँठ

knowledge - (m) ज्ञान, बोध, विद्या

L

labor - (m) श्रम, परिश्रम, (f) मेहनत

laborer - (m) मज़दूर

lack - (m) अभाव, (f) कमी

ladder - (f) सीढ़ी

lady - (f) स्त्री, महिला

lake - (f) झील

lameness (limp) - (f) लँगड़ाहट

lamp - (m) दीपक

land - (f) धरती, भूमि, ज़मीन

landlady - (f) मकान मालकिन

landlord - (m) ज़मींदार, मकान मालिक

lane (alley) - (f) गली

language - (f) भाषा, ज़बान

lap - (f) गोद

lattice - (m) जंगला

latrine - (m) मूत्रालय, शौचालय

laughter - (f) हँसी

launderer - (m) धोबी, (f) धोबिन

law - (m) कानून

lawyer - (m) वकील

laziness - (m) आलस्

leader - (m) नेता

leaf - (m) पत्ता, (f) पत्ती

leaf (plate) - (f) पत्तल

leak - (m) छिद्र, छेद, सूराख

learned one - (m) विद्वान

leather - (m) चमड़ा

lecture - (m) व्याख्यान, भाषण

lecturer - (m) प्राध्यापक, प्रवक्ता

leg - (f) टाँग

leisure - (f) फुर्सत, (m) अवकाश

leisure (time) - (m) फुर्सत

lemon - (m) नींबू, निम्बू

length - (f) लंबाई

lentil - (f) दाल

leopard - (m) चीता

letter - (m) पत्र, (f) चिट्ठी

letter (alphabet) - (m) वर्ण, अक्षर

level - (m) स्तर

library - (m) पुस्तकालय

lid - (m) ढक्कन

lie - (m) झूठ

life - (m) जीवन, जान, (f) ज़िन्दगी

life cycle - (m) जीवन चक्र

life history - (f) जीवन का इतिहास

lifetime - (m) जीवन काल

light - (m) प्रकाश, ज्योति

lightning - (f) बिजली, विद्युत

liking - (f) पसन्द

lily - (m) कुमुद

limb - (m) अंग, अवयव

limestone - (m) चूना

limit - (f) सीमा, हद

line - (f) रेखा

lion - (m) शेर, सिंह

lip - (m) ओठ

liquidity (fluid) - (m) तरल

literature - (m) साहित्य

liver - (m) जिगर

lizard - (f) छिपकली

loan - (m) उधार

lock - (m) ताला

logic - (m) तर्क

loneliness - (m) अकेलापन

looks - (f) शक्ल

lord - (m) प्रभु, भगवन, स्वामी

loss - (f) हानि

lotus - (m) कमल, पंकज, पद्म

love - (m) प्रेम, प्यार, (f) स्नेह

lover - (m) प्रेमी, (f) प्रेमिका, प्रेयसी

luck - (m) भाग्य, (f) किस्मत

luggage - (m) सामान

lullaby - (f) लोरी

lump - (m) डला, देला

lung - (m) फेफड़ा

luxury - (m) विलास

M

machine - (m) यन्त्र

madam - (f) महोदया

magic - (m) जादू

magician - (m) जादूगर

magnet - (m) चुम्बक

mail - (f) डाक

majesty - (m) ऐश्वर्य

majority - (m) अधिकांश

male - (m) नर, पुरुष

man - (m) आदमी, मनुष्य

management - (m) प्रबन्ध

mango - (m) आम

manifestation - (m) अभिव्यक्ति

manner - (m) प्रकार, ढंग, तरीक़ा, (f) तरह, भाँति

manners - (m) शिष्टाचार, (f) तमीज़

mansion - (f) हवेली

mantra - (m) मन्त्र

manure - (m) गोबर

map - (m) नक्शा

marble - (m) संगमरमर

mare - (f) घोड़ी

mark - (m) निशाना

marketplace - (m) बाज़ार

marriage - (f) शादी, (m) विवाह

mason - (m) मिस्त्री

masonry - (f) चुनाई

master - (m) मालिक, (f) मालकिन

mat - (f) चटाई

match(es) - (f) दीयासलाई

mate - (m) यार, मित्र, दोस्त

matter - (m) मामला, (f) बात

mattress - (m) गद्दा

maturity - (f) परिपक्वता

meadow - (m) घास का मैदान

meal - (m) भोजन

meaning - (m) मतलब, अर्थ, तात्पर्य

measurement - (f) नाप

meat - (m) माँस, गोश्त

medicine - (m) औषध, (f) दवाई

meeting - (f) मुलाक़ात, सभा

member - (m) सदस्य

memory - (f) याद, स्मृति

mercy - (m) दया, तरस

merit - (m) गुण, (f) उत्कृष्टता

mess (muddle) - (f) गड़बड़

messenger - (m) दूत

metal - (f) धातु

method - (f) रीति, (m) ढँग, प्रक्रिया

midday - (m) दोपहर

middle - (m) मध्यम

midnight - (f) आधी रात

mildew - (f) फफूंद, भकड़ी

military - (m) सेना

milk - (m) दूध

millionaire - (m) लाखपति

mind - (m) मन

minister - (m) मंत्री

mint - (m) पुदीना

miracle - (m) चमत्कार

mirror - (m) दर्पण, शीशा

mischief - (m) शरारत, (f) शैतानी

miser - (m) कंजूस

misfortune - (m) दुर्भाग्य,
 (f) मुसीबत, अभाग्य

Miss - (f) कुमारी

mist - (m) धुंध, कोहरा

mistake - (f) भूल, गलती, त्रुटि

Mister - (m) श्री, श्रीमान,
 महोदय

mixture - (m) सम्मिश्रण, मेल

mode - (m) तरीका,
 (f) विधा, पद्धति

moderation - (m) संयम

mold - (f) फफूंद, भकड़ी

moment - (m) क्षण, पल

money - (m) पैसा, धन, दौलत

monk - (m) संयासी, मुनि

monkey - (m) बन्दर

month - (m) मास, महीना

mood - (m) मिज़ाज, तबीयत

moon - (m) चंद्र, चाँद

morning - (m) सवेरा, सुबह

mosque - (f) मसजिद

mosquito - (m) मच्छर

moth - (m) पतंगा

mother - (f) माँ, माता

motion - (f) गति

motive - (m) निमित्त

mountain - (m) पहाड़, पर्वत

mouse - (m) चूहा, (f) चुहिया

mouth - (m) मुँह, मुख

Mrs. - (f) श्रीमती

mud - (m) कीचड़

mule - (m) खच्चर, (f) खच्चरी

murder - (f) हत्या, (m) वध

muscle - (f) मांसपेशी

music - (m) संगीत

musician - (m) गायक, संगीतज्ञ

mustache - (f) मूँछ

mustard - (f) सरसों, राई

mystery - (m) रहस्य, भेद

N

nail - (m) कील, मेख

nail (finger) - (m) नाखून

name - (m) नाम

narrow mind - (m) संकीर्णता, संकुचित मन

nation - (m) राष्ट्र

nationality - (f) राष्ट्रीयता

nature - (f) प्रकृति, (m) स्वभाव

nausea - (f) मतली, मिचली, उलटी

nearness - (m) निकटतम, (f) समीपता

necessity - (f) ज़रूरत, आवश्यकता

neck - (f) गर्दन, (m) कण्ठ

nectar - (f) अमृत

need - (f) आवश्यकता, ज़रूरत

needle - (f) सुई

neglect - (m) उपेक्षा

neighbor - (m) पड़ोसी

neighborhood - (m) पड़ोस

nephew - (m) भतीजा, भांजा

nerve - (f) तन्त्रिका

nervous system - (m) तंत्र

nest - (m) घोंसला, नीड़

net - (m) जाल

neutrality - (f) तटस्थता

news - (f) ख़बर, (m) समाचार

newspaper - (m) समाचार पत्र, अख़बार

night - (f) रात, रात्रि, निशा, रजनी

noble - (m) अभिजात

noise - (m) शोर

non-violence - (m) अहिंसा

noose - (m) फंदा, पाश

nose - (m) नाक

noun - (f) संज्ञा

number - (f) सँख्या

nutmeg - (m) जायफल

O

oath - (m) शपथ

object - (f) चीज़, वस्तु (m) पदार्थ

objection - (m) विरोध

obligation - (m) आभार, अनुग्रह

observation - (m) निरीक्षण, प्रेक्षण

observer - (m) निरीक्षक, प्रेक्षक

obstacle - (m) विघ्न

obstruction - (f) रुकावट

occasion - (m) अवसर, मौका

occasion (time) - (f) दफ़ा, बार

ocean - (m) सागर, समुद्र, सिन्धु

offer - (m) प्रस्ताव

offering - (m) अर्पण, (f) भेंट

office - (m) दफ़्तर

official - (m) अधिकारी

oil - (m) तेल

ointment - (m) मलहम

old age - (m) बुढ़ापा

old man - (m) बूढ़ा आदमी

old woman - (f) बूढ़ी महिला

oneness - (f) एकता, अभिन्नता

opinion - (m) मत, विचार, ख्याल

opportunity - (m) अवसर, मौका

opposition - (m) खिलाफ़, विरोध, (f) प्रतिकूलता

orange - (m) संतरा

orchard - (m) बगीचा

order (arrangement) - (m) क्रम, (f) व्यवस्था

order (command) - (f) आज्ञा, (m) हुक्म, आदेश

organization - (m) प्रबन्ध

ostrich - (m) शुतुरमुर्ग

owl - (m) उल्लू

owner - (m) मालिक

ox - (m) बैल

P

package - (f) गठरी, (m) पुलंदा

page - (m) पृष्ठ, पन्ना

pail - (f) बाल्टी

pain (mental) - (m) दुःख

pain (physical) - (m) दर्द, (f) पीड़ा

paint - (m) रंग, रोगन

pair - (m) जोड़ा, (f) जोड़ी

palace - (m) महल

palate - (m) तालू

palm - (f) हथेली

papaya - (f) पपीता

paper - (m) कागज़

paradise - (m) स्वर्ग, आनन्दधाम

paragraph - (m) अनुच्छेद

parents - (m) माता-पिता, माँ-बाप

parrot - (m) तोता

part - (m) भाग, अंश

partner - (m) साझेदार

partnership - (f) साझेदारी

passage (of time) - (m) गुज़र

passenger - (f) सवारी

passion - (m) जोश

past - (m) भूत

past tense - (m) भूत काल

path - (m) रास्ता, मार्ग

patience - (m) धैर्य, धीरज

patient - (m) मरीज़, रोगी

pattern - (m) ढाँचा

paw - (m) पंजा

pea (green) - (m) मटर

peace - (f) शान्ति

peach - (m) आड़ू

peacock - (m) मोर

peak (mountain top) - (m) शिखर

peanut - (f) मूँगफली

pear - (f) नाशपाती

pearl - (m) मोती

pen - (f) कलम

penis - (m) लिंग

people - (m.pl.) लोग

pepper (black) - (f) काली मिर्च

perception - (m) बोध

perfection - (f) पूर्णता

period (of time) - (m) समय, काल, (f) अवधि

permanence - (m) स्थायित्व

persistence - (m) आग्रह

person - (m) व्यक्ति

personality - (m) व्यक्तित्व

perspiration - (m) पसीना

philosophy - (m) दर्शन

pickle - (m) अचार

picture - (f) तस्वीर, चित्र

piece - (m) टुकड़ा

pig - (m) सुअर

pigeon - (m) कबूतर

pile - (m) समूह, ढेर

pill - (f) गोली

pillow - (m) तकिया

pin - (f) सूई

pinch - (f) चुटकी

pipe - (f) नली

pistachio - (m) पिस्ता

pit - (m) गड्ढा

pitcher - (m) घड़ा

place - (f) जगह, (m) स्थान

plan - (f) योजना, उपाय

planet - (m) ग्रह

plank (of wood) - (m) तख्ता

plant - (m) पौधा

plate - (f) थाली

play (child's) - (m) खेल

play (drama) - (m) नाटक

player (sportsman) - (m) खिलाड़ी

pleasure - (m) मज़ा, प्रसन्नता, (f) खुशी

plural - (m) बहुवचन

pocket - (f) जेब

poem - (f) कविता

poet - (m) कवि

point - (m) बिन्दु

point of view - (m) दृष्टिकोण

poison - (m) विष

pole - (m) लम्बा डंडा

policy - (f) नीति

politeness - (f) शिष्टता

pond - (m) तालाब

pool - (m) तालाब

population - (f) आबादी, जनसँख्या

porch - (m) बरामदा

pore - (m) रोम

portion - (m) खण्ड, हिस्सा

pose - (f) मुद्रा

position - (m) पद

possibility - (f) संभावना

post - (m) खम्भा

post office - (m) डाकघर

postposition - (m) कारक

pot - (m) बर्तन

potato - (m) आलू

potter - (m) कुम्हार

poverty - (f) दरिद्रता, गरीबी

powder - (m) चूर्ण

power (force) - (m) बल, ज़ोर, (f) शक्ति

practice - (m) अभ्यास

praise - (f) प्रशंसा, (m) गुण-गान

prayer - (f) प्रार्थना, बिनती

preference - (f) मर्ज़ी, पसन्द

pregnancy - (f) गर्भावस्था

preparation - (f) तैयारी

presence - (f) उपस्थिति

present (gift) - (m) उपहार, (f) भेंट

present (time) - (m) वर्तमान

presentation - (f) प्रस्तुति

president - (m) राष्ट्रपति

pressure - (f) दबाव

prestige - (f) प्रतिष्ठा

price - (f) कीमत, (m) दाम

pride - (m) अभिमान, गर्व

prime minister - (m) प्रधान मंत्री

prince - (m) राजकुमार

princess - (f) राजकुमारी

prisoner - (m) बंदी

privilege - (m) अधिकार

prize - (m) पुरस्कार, इनाम

problem - (f) समस्या

procedure - (f) प्रक्रिया

process - (f) प्रणाली, प्रक्रिया

proclamation - (f) घोषणा

professor - (m) आचार्य

profit - (m) लाभ

progeny - (f) संतान

program - (m) कार्यक्रम

progress - (f) उन्नति

project - (m) कार्य, (f) योजना

promise - (m) वचन, (f) प्रतिज्ञा

pronoun - (m) सर्वनाम

pronunciation - (m) उच्चारण

proof - (m) प्रमाण, (f) परीक्षा

proposal - (m) प्रस्ताव

protection - (m) बचाव, (f) रक्षा, सुरक्षा, शरण

province - (m) प्रदेश

public - (f) जनता

pulse - (f) नाड़ी

pumpkin - (m) कद्दू

punctuality - (f) समय की पाबंदी

punishment - (m) दण्ड

pupil (eye) - (f) (आँख की) पुतली

pupil (student) - (m) शिष्य, छात्र, (f) शिष्या, छात्रा

puppet - (m) पुतला

puppy - (m) पिल्ला, (f) पिल्ली

purification - (m) शोधन, (f) शुद्धि

purity - (f) शुद्धता, शुचिता, पवित्रता

purpose - (m) उद्देश्य, लक्ष्य

purse - (m) बटुवा

push - (m) धक्का

Q

qualification - (f) योग्यता

quality - (m) गुण

quantity - (f) राशि

quarrel - (m) झगड़ा

quarter (1/4) - (f) चौथाई

queen - (f) रानी, बेगम

quest - (f) खोज

question - (m) प्रश्न, सवाल

quickness - (f) स्फूर्ति, शीघ्रता

quilt - (f) रज़ाई

R

rabbit - (m) खरगोश

race - (f) दौड़

race (human) - (f) जाति, प्रजाति

radiance - (f) कान्ति

rain - (f) वर्षा, बारिश

rainbow - (m) इन्द्रधनुष

rainy season - (f) बरसात

raisin - (f) किशमिश

rat - (m) चूहा

ray - (f) किरण

readiness - (f) तैयारी

reality - (f) सच्चाई

realization - (m) साक्षात्कार

reason - (m) कारण, हेतु

reason (logic) - (m) तर्क

recipe - (m) बनाने का तरीका, नुसखा

recluse - (m) साधु, सन्यासी

recognition - (m) पहचान, अभिज्ञान

recommendation - (f) सिफ़ारिश

recreation - (m) मनोविनोद

reflection - (m) प्रतिबिम्ब, (f) परछाई

refreshment - (m) अल्पाहार, जलपान

refuge - (f) शरण

refusal - (m) इन्कार, (f) नकार

region - (m) प्रदेश

regret - (m) खेद, अफ़्सोस, पछतावा

reign - (m) राज्य, शासन

relationship - (m) सम्बंध

relative - (m) संबंधी, रिश्तेदार

relaxation - (m) आराम

relief - (f) राहत

religion - (m) धर्म

relish - (m) स्वाद, मज़ा

remainder - (m) शेष

remains - (m) अवशेष

remedy - (m) उपाय, समाधान

rent - (m) किराया, भाड़ा

renunciation - (m) त्याग

reply - (m) उत्तर, ज़वाब

reputation (fame) - (f) यश

request - (m) निवेदन,
   (f) प्रार्थना, माँग

research - (m) अनुसंधान

residence - (m) निवास

resident - (m) निवासी

respect - (m) आदर, सम्मान,
   (f) इज़्ज़त

responsibility - (m) उत्तरदायित्व,
   (f) ज़िम्मेदारी

rest - (m) विश्राम, आराम

result - (m) परिणाम, नतीजा

reunion (meeting) - (m) मिलन,
   (f) गोष्ठी

reward - (m) इनाम

rhinoceros - (m) गैंडा

rhyme - (f) तुक

rhythm - (f) लय, (m) ताल

rice - (m) चावल

riches - (f) दौलत

ride - (f) सवारी

right - (m) अधिकार

ring (finger) - (f) अँगूठी

river - (f) नदी

road - (m) रास्ता, (f) सड़क

roaming - (m) पर्यटन

rock - (m) पत्थर, शिला

rolling pin - (m) बेलन

roof - (f) छत

room - (m) कमरा

room (space) - (m) जगह

root - (m) मूल, जड़

rope - (f) रस्सी

rose - (m) गुलाब

row - (f) पंक्ति

rug - (m) गलीचा

ruin - (m) नाश, विनाश,
   (f) बरबादी

rule - (m) नियम

rust - (m) ज़ंग

S

saadhak - (m) साधक

saadhanaa - (m) साधना

sack - (m) बोरा, (f) बोरी

sacrifice - (f) कुरबानी

saddle - (m) जीन

safety - (f) रक्षा

saffron - (m) केसर

sage - (m) ऋषि

saint - (m) सन्त, महात्मा

salary - (m) वेतन

salt - (m) नमक

salutation - (m) प्रणाम, अभिवादन, नमस्कार

sand - (m) रेत, रेता

sandalwood - (m) चन्दन

sap - (f) रस

sapphire - (f) नीलम, नीलमणि

sarcasm - (m) व्यंग

satisfaction - (m) संतोष

sauce - (f) चटनी

saw - (f) आरी

sawdust - (m) बुरादा

scaffolding - (m) पाइट

scale - (m) तराजू

scarf - (m) दुपट्टा

scene - (m) दृश्य

scent - (m) खुशबू, सुगन्ध, महक

schedule - (m) कार्यक्रम, (f) सूची, अनुसूची, तालिका

scholar - (m) विद्वान

school - (f) पाठशाला, (m) विद्यालय

science - (m) विज्ञान

scientist - (m) वैज्ञानिक, विज्ञानी

scissors - (f) कैंची

scorpion - (m) बिच्छू

scoundrel - (m) बदमाश

screen - (f) जाली

screw - (m) पेच

sea - (m) समुद्र

sea-level - (m) समुद्र तल

search - (f) तलाश

season - (f) ऋतु

seat - (m) आसन

secret - (f) रहस्य, (m) भेद, राज़

security - (m) सुरक्षा

seed - (m) बीज

selection - (m) चुनाव

self - (m) स्व, (f) आत्मा

seniority - (f) ज्येष्ठता

sense - (f) इन्द्रिय

sense (understanding) - (m) अक़्ल

sentence - (m) वाक्य

sentiment - (m) भाव

seriousness - (f) गंभीरता

sermon - (m) प्रवचन

servant - (m) नौकर, दास, (f) नौकरानी

service - (f) सेवा, नौकरी

sesame - (m) तिल

session - (f) बैठक

sewer - (f) गंदी नाली

sex (gender) - (m) लिंग

shade - (f) छाया	simplicity - (f) सादगी
shadow - (f) छाया, परछाई	sin - (m) पाप
shame - (f) लज्जा, शर्म	singer - (m) गायक
shape - (m) आकार, (f) शक्ल	sir - (m) श्रीमान, महोदय, साहब
share - (m) हिस्सा	sister - (f) बहन, बहिन
sheep - (m) भेड़	sitting - (f) बैठक
sheet - (f) चादर	situation - (f) स्थिति
ship - (m) जहाज़	skill - (f) कुशलता
shirt - (f) कमीज़, (m) कुर्ता	skin - (f) त्वचा, चमड़ी
shock - (m) धक्का	skull - (m) कपाल
shoe - (m) जूता	sky - (m) आकाश, आसमान,
shop - (f) दुकान	गगन, नभ
shop keeper - (m) दुकानदार	slap - (m) थप्पड़, चांटा
shore - (m) किनारा	sleep - (f) नींद
shortage - (f) कमी, (m) अभाव	slug - (m) घोंघा
shoulder - (m) कंधा	smell - (f) गंध
shout (shriek) - (f) चीख़	smell (bad) - (f) बदबू
shovel - (m) बेलचा	smell (good) - (f) खुशबू
show, spectacle - (m) तमाशा	smile - (f) मुस्कुराहट
sickness - (f) बीमारी	smoke - (m) धुआँ
side - (m) पक्ष	smoking - (m) धूम्रपान
sight - (f) नज़र, दृष्टि	snack - (m) उपाहार
sign - (m) चिन्ह, (f) निशानी	snail - (m) घोंघा
signature - (m) हस्ताक्षर,	snake - (m) साँप, सर्प
दस्तख़त	snow - (f) बर्फ़, (m) हिम
significance - (m) महत्व	snowfall - (m) हिमपात
silence - (m) मौन	soap - (m) साबुन
silk - (m) रेशम	society - (m) समाज
silver - (f) चाँदी	sock - (m) मोजा, जुर्राब

soldier - (m) सिपाही, सैनिक

sole (shoe) - (m) तला

solution - (m) समाधान, हल

son - (m) बेटा

song - (m) गीत

sorrow - (m) शोक, खेद

soul - (f) आत्मा

sound - (m) शब्द, (f) ध्वनि

source - (m) उद्गम, स्रोत

south - (m) दक्षिण

space - (m) आकाश

spark - (f) चिनगारी

speaker - (m) बोलने वाला, वक्ता

specialty - (f) विशेषता

speech - (m) भाषण, वचन

speech (spiritual) - (m) प्रवचन

speed (motion) - (f) गति

spice - (m) मसाला

spider - (f) मकड़ी

spine - (f) रीढ़

spinach - (m) पालक

spirit - (f) आत्मा

spirituality - (f) आध्यात्मिकता

splendor - (f) छवि, (m) शान

spoon - (m) चम्मच

spring - (m) बसन्त

sprout - (m) अंकुर

spy - (m) जासूस

squirrel - (f) गिलहरी

stain - (m) दाग़

stairs - (f.pl.) सीढ़ियाँ

stamp (postal) - (m) डाक टिकट

star - (f) तारा, (m) सितारा

state - (f) स्थिति, (m) अवस्था

statue - (f) मूर्ति

steam - (f) भाप

step (foot) - (m) पद, कदम, पग

step (stair) - (f) सीढ़ी

stick - (f) लाठी, (m) डंडा

sting - (m) डंक

stomach - (m) पेट, उदर

stone - (m) पत्थर

stop - (m) रुकावट

store - (f) दुकान

storehouse - (m) भँडार, गोदाम

storm - (m) तूफ़ान

story - (f) कहानी, कथा

storey (floor) - (f) मंजिल

stove - (m) चूल्हा

straw - (m) तिनका

stream - (f) धारा, सरिता

street - (m) सड़क

strength - (m) बल, ज़ोर (f) ताकत,

stretch - (f) अँगड़ाई

string - (f) रस्सी, सुतली

stripe - (f) धारी

struggle - (m) संघर्ष

student - (m) विद्यार्थी, छात्र

study - (m) अध्ययन, पठन,
　(f) पढ़ाई

stump - (m) ठूँठ

style - (f) शैली, रीति, (m) ढँग

subject - (m) विषय

subtlety - (f) सूक्ष्मता

success - (f) सफलता

sugar - (f) चीनी

suggestion - (m) सुझाव

summer - (f) गर्मी (का मौसम)

summit - (m) शिखर

sun - (m) सूरज, सूर्य

sunflower - (m) सूर्यमुखी

sunshine - (f) धूप

supervision - (f) देखभाल

surety - (m) यकीन

surface - (m) तल

surprise - (m) आश्चर्य

surroundings - (m.pl.) आस-पास

suspicion - (f) संदिग्धता

swami - (m) स्वामी

swan - (m) हंस

sweat - (m) पसीना

sweet - (f) मिठाई

sweet potato - (m) शकरकन्दी

sweetheart - (m) प्रेमी, सनम,
　(f) प्रेमिका

swelling - (f) सूजन

symbol - (m) प्रतीक

sympathy - (f) सहानुभूति,
　संवेदना

symposium - (f) गोष्ठी

system - (f) प्रणाली

T

table - (f) मेज़

tail - (f) पूँछ

tailor - (m) दर्ज़ी

talk - (f) बात

talk (idle) - (m) बकवास

tamarind - (f) इमली

tank - (m) तालाब, (f) टंकी

tap - (m) नलका

tape measure - (m) फ़ीता

target - (m) लक्ष्य

taste - (m) स्वाद

tea - (f) चाय

teacher - (m) अध्यापक, शिक्षक,
　(f) अध्यापिका

team - (f) मंडली

technique - (f) विधि, तरीका

telegram - (m) तार

temperament - (m) स्वभाव

temperature - (m) तापमान

temple - (m) मंदिर

tendency - (f) प्रवृत्ति

tense (grammar) - (m) काल

tension - (m) तनाव

territory - (m) इलाक़ा, प्रदेश

terror - (m) त्रास

test - (f) परीक्षा

thanks - (m) धन्यवाद, शुक्रिया

theft - (f) चोरी

theory - (m) सिद्धान्त

thief - (f) चोर

thigh - (f) जाँघ

thing - (f) चीज़, वस्तु, (m) पदार्थ

thing (abstract) - (f) बात

thirst - (f) प्यास

thorn - (m) काँटा

thought - (m) विचार, चिन्तन

thread - (m) सूत्र, धागा

threat - (f) धमकी

throat - (m) गला, कण्ठ

throne - (m) सिंहासन, राजसिंहासन

thumb - (m) अंगूठा

thunder - (f) गर्जन

ticket - (m) टिकट

tiger - (m) बाघ

time - (m) समय, वक्त

time (passed) - (m) अरसा

time(s) - (f) बार, दफ़ा

tin - (m) राँगा

tip - (f) नोक

title - (f) उपाधि

today - (m) आज

toe - (f) पाँव की उँगली

toilet - (m) शौचालय

tolerance - (f) सहनशक्ति

tomato - (m) टमाटर

tomorrow - (m) कल

tomb - (f) कब्र

tone - (m) स्वर, (f) तान

tongue - (f) जिह्वा, ज़बान

tooth - (m) दाँत

top - (m) शीर्ष, (f) चोटी

topic - (m) विषय

torture - (f) यंत्रणा, यातना

total - (m) सम्पूर्ण

touch - (m) स्पर्श

towel - (m) तौलिया

tower - (m) मीनार

town - (m) नगर, शहर

toy - (m) खिलौना

tradition - (f) परम्परा

train - (f) रेल गाड़ी

transaction - (m) संचालन

transformation - (m) परिवर्तन

translation - (m) भाषांतर, अनुवाद

trap - (m) फंदा, जाल

trash - (m) कूड़ा

travel - (f) यात्रा, (m) सफर,

traveler - (f) यात्री, (m) मुसाफ़िर,

treasure - (f) निधि, दौलत

treasury - (m) कोष, खजाना

treatment - (m) आचरण, व्यवहार

tree - (m) वृक्ष, पेड़

trellis - (f) जाली

triangle - (m) त्रिकोण, त्रिभुज

trick - (f) चालाकी

trip - (f) यात्रा, सफ़र

triumph - (m) विजय, जीत

trouble - (f) परेशानी, मुसीबत, तकलीफ़, (m) कष्ट

trousers - (m) पतलून

trunk (car) - (f) डिक्की

trust - (m) विश्वास

truth - (m) सच, सत्य

tube - (f) नाली

tune (note) - (m) सुर, राग

turban - (f) पगड़ी

turmeric - (f) हलदी

turn (in a road) - (m) मोड़

turn (opportunity) - (f) बारी

turnip - (m) शलगम

turquoise - (m) फ़ीरोज़ा

twilight - (f) सांझ

twist - (f) ऐंठन

type - (f) शैली, (m) नमूना, प्रकार, ढंग

U

umbrella - (f) छतरी, (m) छाता

unconsciousness - (f) बेहोशी

uneasiness - (f) बेचैनी

union - (m) मिलन, सम्मिलन, संयोग

unity - (m) एकत्व, (f) युक्ति

universe - (m) विश्व

university - (m) विश्वविद्यालय

upstairs - (f) ऊपरी मंज़िल

use - (m) उपयोग, प्रयोग, इस्तेमाल

V

vacation - (f) छुट्टी

valley - (f) घाटी

value - (m) मूल्य, कीमत

vanity - (m) दंभ

vapor - (m) वाष्प, भाप

variation - (m) परिवर्तन

variety - (f) विभिन्नता

vase - (m) फूलदान

vegetable - (f) सब्ज़ी

vegetables (cooked) - (f) सब्ज़ी तरकारी

vegetarian - (m) शाकाहारी

vegetation - (f) हरियाली

vehicle - (f) गाड़ी

veil - (m) पर्दा

veil of ignorance - (m) आवरण

vein - (f) नाड़ी

verandah - (m) बरामदा

verb - (f) क्रिया

verification - (f) जांच

verse - (m) पद

vibration - (m) स्फुरण, स्पन्दन, कम्पन

victim - (m) शिकार

victory - (f) विजय, जीत

view - (m) दृश्य, अवलोकन

view (point of ~) - (m) दृष्टिकोण

village - (m) गाँव, ग्राम

villager - (m) गाँव वाला, ग्रामीण

villain (rogue) - (m) बदमाश

vine - (f) लता, बेल

vinegar - (m) सिरका

violation - (m) उल्लंघन

violence - (f) हिंसा

virtue - (m) गुण

visibility - (f) दिखाई

vision - (f) दृष्टि

visitor - (f) अतिथि, (m) मेहमान

voice - (f) आवाज़, वाणी

volcano - (m) ज्वालामुखी

vow - (m) वादा, शपथ

vowel - (m) स्वर

voyage - (f) यात्रा

W

wage - (f) मज़दूरी, (m) वेतन

waist - (f) कमर

wall - (f) दीवार

wallet - (m) बटुवा

walnut - (m) अखरोट

war - (m) युद्ध

warehouse - (m) गोदाम

warning - (f) चेतावनी

washerman - (m) धोबी

washerwoman - (f) धोबिन

waste - (m) क्षय, (f) बरबादी

watch - (f) घड़ी

water - (m) पानी, जल

waterfall - (m) झरना

watermelon - (m) तरबूज़

wave - (f) लहर, तरंग

wax - (m) मोम

way - (m) ढँग, पथ, प्रकार, (f) पद्धति, विधि

weakness - (f) दुर्बलता, कमज़ोरी

wealth - (m) धन

weapon - (m) शास्त्र

weather - (m) मौसम

web - (m) जाला

weed - (m) घास

week - (m) सप्ताह, हफ़्ता

weight - (m) वज़न, भार, (f) तौल

welcome - (m) स्वागत

welfare - (m) हित

well being - (m) हित

well wisher - (m)
हित की बात सोचने वाला

west - (m) पश्चिम

wheat - (m) गेहूँ

wheel - (m) चक्र

whip - (m) चाबुक

whirlpool - (m) भँवर

whisper - (f) खुसर-फुसर,
फुसफुसाहट

whistle - (f) सीटी

wick - (f) बत्ती

widow - (f) विधवा

width - (f) चौड़ाई

wife - (f) पत्नी

wind - (f) हवा, वायु, (m) पवन

window - (f) खिड़की

wing - (m) पंख

winner - (m) जीतनेवाला,
विजेता

winter - (f) सर्दी (m) जाड़ा

wire - (m) तार

wisdom - (m) ज्ञान, (f) बुद्धिमानी

wish - (f) चाह, इच्छा,
अभिलाषा, मर्ज़ी

witness - (m) गवाह, साक्षी, दर्शक,
(f) गवाही

wok - (f) कड़ाही

wolf - (m) भेड़िया

woman - (f) महिला, स्त्री,
औरत, नारी

womb - (m) गर्भ

wonder - (m) आश्चर्य

wood - (f) लकड़ी

wool - (m) ऊन

word - (m) शब्द

work - (m) काम, श्रम, कार्य

work (hard) - (m) कठिन मेहनत,
परिश्रम

world - (f) दुनिया, (m) जगत,
संसार

worm - (m) कीड़ा

worry - (f) चिन्ता, फ़िक्र

worship - (f) आरती, पूजा,
आराधना, अर्चना

worth - (m) मूल्य, महत्त्व,
(f) योग्यता

wound - (m) ज़ख़्म, (f) चोट

wreath - (f) माला

wrinkle - (f) झुर्री

wrist - (f) कलाई

writer - (m) लेखक

wrong - (f) गलती, त्रुटि

Y

yawn - (f) जँभाई
year - (m) वर्ष, साल
yog - (m) योग
yogi - (m) योगी
yogini - (f) योगिनी
yogurt - (m) दही
young man - (m) नौजवान, युवक
young woman - (f) युवती
youth - (m) यौवन, युवक

Z

zeal - (m) उत्साह, जोश
zero - (m) शून्य
zodiac - (m) राशि-चक्र
zodiacal sign - (f) राशि
zone - (m) घेरा

Postpositions

In English, prepositions precede their objects. Their counter-parts in Hindi are called postpositions, because they are positioned <u>after</u> their object.

Simple Postpositions

There are five simple postpositions which consist of one word: से 'by, from, with'; में 'in'; पर 'on, at'; को 'to'; and तक 'up to, as far as':

पानी में	<u>in</u> the water
मेज़ पर	<u>on</u> the table
चाकू से	<u>with</u> the knife[1]

Do not forget that when a postposition follows a noun, the noun must be put in the oblique case, and an adjective ending in आ describing the noun usually reflects the oblique case of the noun:

अच्छे कमरे में   in the good room

Simple postpositions are used with pronouns in their oblique form (see Pronouns pg. 27):

मुझसे	from me
इस पर	on this
उनको	to them

---

[1] When the postposition से means 'with,' the sense is instrumental (e.g., कलम से 'with a pen'). To convey the sense of accompaniment, the postposition के साथ is used (e.g., आदमी के साथ 'with the man').

Compound Postpositions

Postpositions consisting of two words usually begin with the word के (although in a few cases they start with की or से):

लड़की के लिए	<u>for</u> the girl
मकान <u>के सामने</u>	<u>in front of</u> the house

When these postpositions are used with pronouns, they take possessive pronouns in their masculine plural or feminine form (see Pronouns: pg. 24), and the के or की is dropped from the postposition:

मेरे लिए	for me
हमारे सामने	in front of us
उसके पास	near him/her/it/that
उनकी तरफ	towards them

The Possessive Postposition (Particle)

The possessive postpositions का, की, के 'of' or 'belonging to,' appearing between the possessor and the object possessed, express possession in the same way as an apostrophe with an 's' does in English. The possessive postposition agrees with the object being possessed in gender and number:

लड़की का कमरा	the girl's room
लड़की की किताब	the girl's book
लड़की के कमरे	the girl's rooms

Being postpositions they require the preceding nouns to take the oblique case:

लड़के का कमरा	the boy's room

86

If the object being possessed is a masculine noun in the oblique case then के is used instead of का:

लड़के के कमरे में   in the boy's room

In this example, the postposition में requires कमरा to take the oblique case (i.e., कमरे); consequently the possessive postposition का becomes के.

Use of जैसा as a Postposition

जैसा is sometimes used as a postposition meaning 'like, similar to'. The preceding noun or pronoun is put in the oblique case, and जैसा agrees with the noun or pronoun it describes:

उन जैसा	like them
कुत्ते जैसा	like a dog
उन जैसे लोग	people like them
उन जैसी लड़कियाँ बहुत पढ़ती हैं ।	Girls like them read a lot.
वह चीते जैसा दौड़ता है ।	He runs like a cheetah.

Uses of से

This postposition is most commonly used to mean 'from,' 'by,' or 'with':

भारत से	from India
रेल गाड़ी से	by train
कैंची से	with scissors

से is also used in references to periods of time, meaning 'since' or 'for':

महेश कल से बीमार है।	Mahaysh has been sick <u>since yesterday</u>.[2]
वह पाँच साल से यहाँ है।	He has been here <u>for five years</u>.
मैंने दो दिनों से खाना नहीं खाया।	I didn't eat <u>for two days</u>.

से can also be used to express cause, sometimes meaning 'because of':

धूप से पत्ते सूख गए।	The leaves dried <u>because of (from) the sun</u>.
लड़का कुत्ते से डरता है।	The boy is afraid <u>(because) of the dog</u>.

The use of से in making comparisons is described in Adjectives (see pg. 33).

---

[2] Literally, 'Mahaysh is sick since yesterday.' It is common to use the present tense of होना for 'has/have been' with this use of से.

Postpositions for 'to have'

There is no verb in Hindi that corresponds to the English verb 'to have.' The sense of possession, ownership, relationship, etc., expressed in the English sentences, 'I have three dollars,' 'He has two brothers,' 'Mary has a little lamb,' and 'I have a feeling,' is expressed in Hindi by means of postpositions. The postposition used depends on the kind or class of thing possessed.

For most physical objects, the postposition के पास (literally, 'near, beside') is used:

करिश्मा के पास दो किताबें हैं ।	Karishmaa has two books.
मेरे पास एक क़लम है ।	I have a pen.
हमारे पास पैसा नहीं है ।	We don't have (any) money.

For relations, parts of the body, and particularly large and immovable physical objects (e.g., houses, orchards, etc.) the possessive pronoun (मेरा, आपका, etc.) or the possessive postposition (का, की, के) is used:

मेरे दो भाई हैं ।	I have two brothers. (Two brothers are mine.)
कजोल के कितने बच्चे हैं ?	How many children does Kajol have?
कुत्ते की लम्बी पूँछ है ।	The dog has a long tail.
हमारा बगीचा है ।	We have an orchard.

For objects of a more abstract or non-material nature, the postposition को is used (see Verbs pg. 119):

हमको समय नहीं है ।	We have no time.
प्रधान मन्त्री को अधिकार है ।	The Prime Minister has the right.
लड़की को जुकाम था ।	The girl had a cold.

Use of को with Direct Objects

Whenever the action of a verb is directed towards a particular animate object (i.e., a person or animal), the object always takes the postposition को unless the specific sense of another postposition is called for:

पिता-जी को बुलाइए ।   Call <u>Father</u>! [3]

मैं <u>आदमी</u> को देखता हूँ ।   I see <u>the man</u>.

When a verb is directed towards a non-specific object, then the object does not take को:

मैं <u>आदमी</u> देखता हूँ ।   I see <u>a man</u>.

In the case of inanimate objects, को is only used when there is a definite requirement to particularize a certain object:

उस किताब को पढ़ो ।   Read that book.

---

[3] Note that को does not have the meaning 'to' in this usage.

A

about - के बारे में
above - के ऊपर
according to - के अनुसार
across - के पार
after - के बाद, के उपरांत
against (opposed) - के विपरीत
ahead of - के आगे
all around - के चारों तरफ
amongst - के बीच में
apart from - के अलावा
around - के करीब
around (in the vicinity) -
   के आस-पास
as far as - तक
at - पर
at the place of - के यहाँ

B

because of - के कारण, के मारे
before - के पहले
behind - के पीछे
below - के नीचे
beneath - के नीचे
beside - के पास
besides - के अलावा
better than - से बढ़कर
beyond - के पार
by (means of) - के द्वारा, से,
   के ज़रिये

C

close, near - के नज़दीक,
   के पास
come in contact - के सम्पर्क में
contrary to - के विपरीत

D

due to - के कारण
during - के बीच में

E

except, excluding - के सिवाय
extra, more than - के अतिरिक्त

F

for - के लिए
for the purpose of - के निमित्त
for the sake of - के निमित्त
from - से

H

has, have (possession) - के पास

I

in - में
in between - के बीच में
in exchange for - के बदले में
in front of - के सामने
in place of - के बदले में
in relation to - के नाते
in spite of - के बावजूद

in the direction of - की तरफ,
की दिशा में

in the form of - के रूप में

including - सहित

inside - के अन्दर

instead of - की बजाय

L

like - के समान, की तरह

like - जैसा (see pg. 87)

like this, in comparison -
की तरह

M

meanwhile - के दौरान

N

near, close - के नज़दीक,
के करीब, के सम्पर्क में

nevertheless - के बावजूद

next to - के पास

no more than -
के अतिरिक्त (नहीं)

O

on - पर

on behalf of - की ओर से

on the side of - के किनारे

on the left side of -
के बायीं तरफ़

on the right side of -
के दायीं तरफ़

on top of - के ऊपर

opposite to - के विपरीत

over - के पार, के ऊपर

P

prior to - के पूर्व

S

similar to - जैसा (see pg. 87)

T

through - के द्वारा

towards - की ओर, की दिशा में

to - को

U

under - के नीचे

until - तक

up to - तक

W

with (accompaniment) -
के साथ

with (instrumental) - से

without - के बिना

worthy of - के योग्य, के लायक

Adverbs

Adverbs are used to modify a verb, adjective, or another adverb. They describe manner, extent, time, or place.

Adverbs that describe the manner in which an action is performed are usually placed close to the verb they modify:

मैं धीरे जाता हूँ ।   I go <u>slowly</u>.

Adverbs of time or place are usually placed at the beginning of the sentence, after the subject:

मैं प्रतिदिन बाज़ार जाता हूँ ।   <u>Everyday</u> I go to the market.

Interrogative Sentences

Interrogative adverbs such as कहाँ 'where,' कब 'when,' कैसे 'how,' and क्यों 'why' are usually placed before the verb:

शेरु कहाँ जा रहा है?   <u>Where</u> is Shayru going?

आप क्यों मुस्कराते हैं?   <u>Why</u> do you smile?

If क्या is the first word of a sentence, then it is a general sign of interrogation and turns the sentence into a question:

क्या पिता-जी जानते हैं ?   <u>Does</u> Father know?

If क्या appears before the verb, it has the meaning 'what' (i.e., it functions as an interrogative pronoun):

आप क्या जानते हैं ?   <u>What</u> do you know?

The adverb न 'no, not' placed at the end of a sentence asks a (possibly rhetorical) question:

वे आज जा रहे हैं न?   They are going today, aren't they?

वह यहाँ काम करता है, है न?   He works here, doesn't he?

वह वहाँ गई न?   She went there, didn't she?

Devices Used to Form Adverbs

The postposition से 'with' is used to form adverbs from nouns, adjectives, and other adverbs:

शान्ति से   quietly, peacefully (शान्ति quiet, peace)

ठीक से   properly (ठीक proper)

धीरे से   slowly (धीरे slowly)

Adding रूप से forms adverbs from certain nouns and adjectives:

विशेष रूप से   especially (विशेष special)

पूर्ण रूप से   completely (पूर्ण whole)

The suffix पूर्वक makes adverbs of manner from nouns:

प्रसन्नता पूर्वक   happily (प्रसन्नता happiness)

आदरपूर्वक   respectfully (आदर respect)

Note: In Hindi, some adverbs and postpositions are related to one another with के or की being used to denote the postposition. Compare the following pairs of sentences:

पीछे देखिए ।   Look behind.
                     (पीछे is an adverb.)

मकान के पीछे देखिए ।   Look behind the house.
                     (के पीछे is a postposition.)

कोमल्ता आगे चली ।   Komaltaa went ahead.

वह आदमी के आगे चला ।   He went ahead of the man.

A

above - ऊपर

abruptly - एक दम से

across - पार

actually - सचमुच, वास्तव में

additionally - और

affectionately - सप्रेम

after all - आख़िर

again - फिर, पुनः, और

again and again - बार बार

ago - पहले, पूर्व

ahead - आगे

all around - चारों-ओर, चारों-तरफ

all day - दिन-भर

almost - लगभग, करीब

along with - सहित, समेत

also - भी

although - हालाँकि

always - सदा, हमेशा

amongst (ourselves) - आपस में

anymore - फिर भी

anyway - खैर

anywhere - कहीं भी

apart - अलग

approximately - लगभग

as, as if - जैसे

as if - मानों

as much as - जितना

as though - मानों

as well - भी

at all - कदापि

at last - आख़िर

at once - एक दम

automatically - अपने आप, स्वतः

awhile - थोड़ी देर के लिए

B

backwards - पीछे

badly - बुरी तरह (से)

barely - चिन्मात्र

before - पहिले, सामने

behind - के पीछे

below - नीचे

beneath - नीचे

besides - और

between - मध्य में, बीच में

beyond - दूर, पार

beyond (a little) - कुछ दूर

both sides - दोनों ओर

brightly - चमाचम

by chance - संयोग से, इत्तफ़ाक़ से

by no means - कदापि नहीं

C

carefully - ध्यान से, सावधानी से

certainly - अवश्य (ही), ज़रूर, बेशक

95

completely - पूरी तरह से, पूर्ण रूप से

constantly - निरन्तर

continuously - लगातार

D

daily - दैनिक, रोज़, प्रति-दिन

day after tomorrow - परसों

day and night - निशिदिन

day before yesterday - परसों

day by day - दिन-ब-दिन

definitely - निश्चय ही, निश्चित रूप से

different places - कहीं-कहीं

difficulty (with) - मुश्किल से, कठिनता से

directly - सीधे, प्रत्यक्षतः

don't - नहीं

don't (with command) - मत

down - नीचे

during - उस दौरान, इस दौरान

E

each other - परस्पर, एक दूसरे से

early - शीघ्र, जल्दी

easily - सहजता से

elsewhere - कहीं और

entirely - बिलकुल

especially - खास तौर से, विशेष रूप से

et cetera - इत्यादि

even - ही

even so - तो भी

even still - फिर भी

eventually - अंत में

everyday - रोज़ रोज़, प्रतिदिन

everywhere - सर्वत्र, हर जगह, सब कहीं

exactly - बिलकुल ठीक

excited - उत्तेजित

extremely - अति, अत्यन्त, बहुत

F

facing - सामने

far - दूर

far enough - काफ़ी दूर

farther - और दूर, आगे

fast - जल्दी, तेज़

finally - अन्ततः

for instance - उदाहरण के लिए

forcefully - विवश होकर, ज़ोर से

forever - हमेशा, सदा

fully - पूर्णतः

further - और

furthermore - और भी

G

generally - अधिकांशतः, साधारणतः

gently - धीरे-धीरे, चुप-चाप

gladly - शौक से

gradually - धीरे-धीरे, आहिस्ता

great (exclamation) - शाबाश

greatly - अत्यन्त

H

happily - खुशी से, सानंद, आनंद से, प्रसन्नता से, प्रसन्नता पूर्वक

hard - ज़ोर से

hardly - शायद ही, मुश्किल से

hence - अतः, इसलिए

here - यहाँ, इधर

high - ऊपर, ऊँचा

how long - कब तक

how much - कितना

however - किसी प्रकार से

I

ideally - आदर्श रूप में

illegally - अवैध रूप से

immediately, at once - तुरन्त, अभी, फ़टाफ़ट

in any way - किसी प्रकार

in fact - वास्तव में

in such a way - ऐसा

in the meantime - इतने में

in the presence of - सामने, उपस्थिति में

in this way - इस प्रकार से, ऐसा

inconvenient - असुविधाजनक

indeed - वस्तुतः, सचमुच

inside - अंदर

intentionally - जान बूझकर

J

just as - जैसे

just like - जैसे

just so - ऐसे ही

K

kindly - कृपया, कृपा करके

knowingly - जान बूझकर, जानकर

L

late - देर से

later - बाद में

left (to the) - बाएँ

likewise - इस प्रकार से

little (while) - तनिक

loudly - ज़ोर से

low - नीचे

luckily - सौभाग्य से

M

maybe - शायद

monthly - मासिक, प्रतिमास

more - और

moreover - फिर

mostly - अधिकांशतः, अधिकतर

mutually - आपस में, परस्पर

N

near - निकट, नज़दीक, पास, समीप

near about - आस-पास

nearby - पास में, कुछ ही दूर

nearest - निकटतम

necessarily - आवश्यक रूप से

never - कभी नहीं, कदापि नहीं

nevertheless - फिर भी, तो भी

next - फिर, दूसरा

nicely - अच्छी तरह से

no - नहीं

not - नहीं

not at all - कदापि नहीं

not only - न केवल

not yet - अभी तक नहीं

now - अब

nowhere - कहीं नहीं

O

of course - बेशक

often - अक्सर

on all sides - चारों ओर

on both sides - दोनों ओर

on that side - उस ओर

on top - ऊपर

once - एक बार, एक दफ़ा

once again - एक बार फिर, एक बार और, दुबारा,

only - केवल, ही, सिर्फ़

only then - केवल, तब ही

opposite - विपरीत

opposite side - उस पार

otherwise - नहीं तो

otherwise - वैसे भी, वरना

outside - बाहर

over - ऊपर

overhead - ऊपर

P

particular - खास तौर पर

perhaps - कदाचित्, शायद

possibly - हो सके तो, यदि सम्भव हो तो

previously - पूर्व से, पहिले से

probably - संभवतः, कदाचित्

properly - ठीक से

punctually - ठीक समय पर

Q

quickly - जल्दी से
quietly - चुपचाप, शान्ति से
quite - बिलकुल, काफ़ी

R

rather - बल्कि
really - सचमुच
regularly - नियमित रूप से
right (to the) - दाएँ
right now - अभी

S

scarcely - शायद ही
slow - धीरे
slowly - धीरे से, आहिस्ता
so - ऐसे
so on - इत्यादि
some time (ahead) -
  अरसे तक
some time (back) -
  अरसे से
somehow - किसी भी तरह,
  जैसे ही
sometime - कभी
sometime (after) -
  कुछ देर के बाद
sometime or other -
  कभी न कभी

somewhere - कहीं
somewhere else - कहीं और
somewhere or other -
  कहीं न कहीं
soon - शीघ्र, थोड़ी देर में
specially - खास तौर पर,
  खासकर
still - फिर, फिर भी
straight - सीधे
suddenly - अचानक, सहसा
suppose - मान लो
sure - अवश्य, ज़रूर

T

that is why - इसीलिए
then - तब, फिर
there - वहाँ, उधर
therefore - इसलिए
these days - आज-कल
though - हालाँकि
thus - इस प्रकार से, ऐसे
today - आज
together - साथ-साथ,
  इकट्ठे, मिलकर
tomorrow - कल,
  आने वाला कल
too - भी
totally - बिलकुल
truly - सचमुच, सचाई से

truthfully - ईमानदारी से,
सच्चाई से

twice - दुबारा

U

ultimately - अन्ततः

unanimously - एक मत से

under - नीचे

unexpectedly - इत्तफ़ाक़ से

unlikely - सम्भवतः नहीं,
शायद नहीं

up - ऊपर

upside down - उलटा-सीधा,
ऊपर-नीचे

usually - सामान्य रूप से,
सामान्यतः

V

very - बहुत, अति

via - (से) होकर

W

well - अच्छी तरह (से)

well! (excl.) - खैर

whenever - जब भी

where - जहाँ, जिधर

wherever - कहीं भी, जहाँ भी

while - (See Verbs pg. 139)

whole (of) - भर

whole day - दिन भर

Y

yesterday - कल, पिछला कल

yet, up till now - अभी तक

Interrogative Adverbs

how - कैसे

how much - कितना

when - कब

where - कहाँ

why - क्यों

Interrogative word - क्या [1]

---

[1] क्या must be placed at the beginning of a sentence to make the sentence a question. (See pg. 93)

Verbs

This chapter begins with a section in which the conjugation of verbs in their most important tenses is given, followed by commonly used constructions, some supplementary notes on verbs, and a dictionary listing of verbs in their infinitive form.

The infinitive form of all verbs ends in ना. Verb forms are made by removing ना, leaving the verb stem (e.g., the stem of देखना is देख). Endings for each tense are added to this stem.

On the following page is a chart, summarizing the tenses, which can be used as a reference to find the name of the tense you are looking for. It shows the third person masculine singular forms of the irregular verb होना 'to be, become' and the regular verb देखना 'to see.'

Generally, verbs are negated by placing नहीं before the verb:

मैं नहीं देखूँगा ।   I will not see.

मैं नहीं जा रहा हूँ ।   I am not going.

Exceptions to this general rule will be noted.

In tenses where the form of a verb differs according to the gender of its subject, the form for a masculine subject is given first, followed by the form for a feminine subject:

मैं देखता हूँ / देखती हूँ ।   I see.

(masc.)   (fem.)

The pronoun वह is translated on the following pages as 'he/she,' though it also has the meanings 'it' and 'that.' Note that the verb forms for the pronouns यह and ये are conjugated in exactly the same way as वह and वे, respectively.

In the dictionary listing, a verb preceded by a postposition in brackets (e.g., का 'of,' से 'from, by') indicates that the object of the verb, if present, must be followed by the given postposition.

101

Summary of Tenses

(shown in the third person masc. sing.)

Infinitive
होना to be   देखना to see

Stem
हो be   देख see

Imperative
हो Be!   देखो, देखिए Look! See!

Imperfect Participle
होता is   देखता sees

Present Imperfect
होता है is   देखता है sees

Past Imperfect
होता था used to be   देखता था used to see

Future Imperfect
होता होगा must be   देखता होगा must see

Present Continuous
हो रहा है is happening   देख रहा है is seeing

Past Continuous
हो रहा था was happening   देख रहा था was seeing

Future Continuous
हो रहा होगा must be happening   देख रहा होगा must be seeing

Future
होगा will be   देखेगा will see

Subjunctive
हो may be   देखे may see

Perfect Participle
हुआ became, happened   देखा saw

Present Perfect
हुआ है has been   देखा है has seen

Past Perfect
हुआ था had been   देखा था had seen

Future Perfect
हुआ होगा must have been   देखा होगा must have seen

102

Forms of होना 'to be'

होना is used on its own or as an auxiliary (helping) verb in the formation of numerous tenses.

PRESENT

मैं हूँ	I am
तू है	you are
वह है	he/she is
हम हैं	we are
तुम हो	you are
आप हैं	you are
वे हैं	they are

PAST

मैं था / थी	I was
तू था / थी	you were
वह था / थी	he/she was
हम थे / थीं	we were
तुम थे / थीं	you were
आप थे / थीं	you were
वे थे / थीं	they were

SUBJUNCTIVE[1]

मैं हूँ	I may (might) be
तू हो	you may (might) be
वह हो	he/she may (might) be
हम हों	we may (might) be
तुम हो	you may (might) be
आप हों	you may (might) be
वे हों	they may (might) be

FUTURE

मैं हूँगा / हूँगी	I will be
तू होगा / होगी	you will be
वह होगा / होगी	he/she will be
हम होंगे / होंगी	we will be
तुम होगे / होगी	you will be
आप होंगे / होंगी	you will be
वे होंगे / होंगी	they will be

PERFECT PARTICIPLE

हुआ (m. sing.) been, happened	हुई (f. sing.) been, happened
हुए (m. pl.) been, happened	हुईं (f. pl.) been, happened

---

[1] In conversation, future tense forms of होना are often used with शायद 'maybe' instead of the subjunctive (e.g., वह शायद यहाँ होगा । He might be here).

PRESENT IMPERFECT

For making general statements, the present imperfect form of होना is used — होता है, होती है, होते हैं, होती हैं.

Compare the following:

कौआ छोटा है ।	The crow is small.
कौए काले होते हैं ।	Crows (in general) are black.
ये आम कच्चे हैं ।	These (particular) mangos are unripe.
पक्के आम मीठे होते हैं ।	Ripe mangos (in general) are sweet.

Imperative

The imperative form of a verb is used to express commands. Two common imperative forms are shown next. One is familiar and used with persons addressed as तुम, while the other is respectful and used with persons one would address as आप:

with तुम		**with आप**	
देखो	Look!	देखिए	Look!
रहो ²	Be!	रहिए	Be!

FOUR VERBS WITH IRREGULAR IMPERATIVE FORMS

		with तुम	**with आप**	
करना	(to do)	करो	कीजिए	Do!
लेना	(to take)	लो	लीजिए	Take!
देना	(to give)	दो	दीजिए	Give!
पीना	(to drink)	पिओ	पीजिए	Drink!

---

² To express the imperative sense of the verb होना, the verb रहना 'to remain' is usually used (e.g., शान्त <u>रहो/रहिए</u> । <u>Be</u> quiet (peaceful)).

The particle मत 'do not, don't' is used before the verb to make the command negative:

मत करो ! मत कीजिए !   Don't do (that)!

The infinitive is also used as an imperative, and is more of a request than a command:

यहाँ आना ।   Come here (please).

The adverb न 'do not, don't' is used before the verb in the infinitive to make the request negative:

यहाँ न आना ।   Do not come here (please).

A further imperative form in which the ending गा is added to the imperative form for आप (e.g., देखिएगा, कीजिएगा, दीजिएगा etc.) is used for polite requests:

कुछ पानी माता-जी को   Kindly give Mother some
दीजिएगा ।   water.

धीरे से बोलिएगा ।   Would you please speak
     slowly.

The Imperfect Tenses

The imperfect tenses describe habitual actions or general states.

Present Imperfect

मैं देखता हूँ / देखती हूँ	I see
तू देखता है / देखती है	you see
वह देखता है / देखती है	he/she sees
हम देखते हैं / देखती हैं	we see
तुम देखते हो / देखती हो	you see
आप देखते हैं / देखती हैं	you see
वे देखते हैं / देखती हैं	they see

In negative statements, नहीं is placed before the verb and हूँ, है, हो, or हैं is normally dropped (e.g., मैं नहीं देखता । I do not see). Moreover, when the subject is feminine plural, the final vowel sound of the verb is nasalized (e.g., वे नहीं देखतीं । They don't see).

PAST IMPERFECT (habitual past)

मैं देखता था / देखती थी	I used to see
तू देखता था / देखती थी	you used to see
वह देखता था / देखती थी	he/she used to see
हम देखते थे / देखती थीं	we used to see
तुम देखते थे / देखती थीं	you used to see
आप देखते थे / देखती थीं	you used to see
वे देखते थे / देखती थीं	they used to see

FUTURE IMPERFECT

This tense expresses assumption or certainty rather than compulsion or obligation.

मैं देखता हूँगा / देखती हूँगी	I must see
तू देखता होगा / देखती होगी	you must see
वह देखता होगा / देखती होगी	he/she must see
हम देखते होंगे / देखती होंगी	we must see
तुम देखते होगे / देखती होगी	you must see
आप देखते होंगे / देखती होंगी	you must see
वे देखते होंगे / देखती होंगी	they must see

106

The Continuous Tenses

The continuous tenses describe actions that are in progress.

PRESENT CONTINUOUS

मैं देख रहा हूँ / रही हूँ	I am seeing
तू देख रहा है / रही है	you are seeing
वह देख रहा है / रही है	he/she is seeing
हम देख रहे हैं / रही हैं	we are seeing
तुम देख रहे हो / रही हो	you are seeing
आप देख रहे हैं / रही हैं	you are seeing
वे देख रहे हैं / रही हैं	they are seeing

PAST CONTINUOUS

मैं देख रहा था / रही थी	I was seeing
तू देख रहा था / रही थी	you were seeing
वह देख रहा था / रही थी	he/she was seeing
हम देख रहे थे / रही थीं	we were seeing
तुम देख रहे थे / रही थीं	you were seeing
आप देख रहे थे / रही थीं	you were seeing
वे देख रहे थे / रही थीं	they were seeing

FUTURE CONTINUOUS

मैं देख रहा हूँगा / रही हूँगी	I will be seeing
तू देख रहा होगा / रही होगी	you will be seeing
वह देख रहा होगा / रही होगी	he/she will be seeing
हम देख रहे होंगे / रही होंगी	we will be seeing
तुम देख रहे होगे / रही होगी	you will be seeing
आप देख रहे होंगे / रही होंगी	you will be seeing
वे देख रहे होंगे / रही होंगी	they will be seeing

Future

मैं देखूँगा / देखूँगी	I will see
तू देखेगा / देखेगी	you will see
वह देखेगा / देखेगी	he/she will see
हम देखेंगे / देखेंगी	we will see
तुम देखोगे / देखोगी	you will see
आप देखेंगे / देखेंगी	you will see
वे देखेंगे / देखेंगी	they will see

Two Verbs with Irregular Future Forms

देना (to give)

मैं दूँगा / दूँगी	I will give
तू देगा / देगी	you will give
वह देगा / देगी	he/she will give
हम देंगे / देंगी	we will give
तुम दोगे / दोगी	you will give
आप देंगे / देंगी	you will give
वे देंगे / देंगी	they will give

लेना (to take)

मैं लूँगा / लूँगी	I will take
तू लेगा / लेगी	you will take
वह लेगा / लेगी	he/she will take
हम लेंगे / लेंगी	we will take
तुम लोगे / लोगी	you will take
आप लेंगे / लेंगी	you will take
वे लेंगे / लेंगी	they will take

Subjunctive

The subjunctive form of a verb is used to express something wished, hoped for, or requested, and suggests that an action is uncertain but possible.

मैं देखूँ	I may (might, should) see
तू देखे	you may (might, should) see
वह देखे	he/she may (might, should) see
हम देखें	we may (might, should) see
तुम देखो	you may (might, should) see
आप देखें	you may (might, should) see
वे देखें	they may (might, should) see

The subjunctive form is made negative using न:

आप यहाँ न बैठें ।	You may not sit here.

The subjunctive mood is illustrated in the following:

आप जल्दी से ठीक हो जाएं ।	May you recover quickly.
आप मुझे क्षमा करें ।	Please excuse me.
क्या मैं आऊँ?	Should I come?
हम क्या करें?	What should we do?
हो सकता है कि वह आए ।	It is possible that he might come.

The subjunctive is also sometimes used in expressions of necessity:

यह आवश्यक है कि हम ठीक समय पर पहुँचें ।	It is necessary that we arrive on time.

The adverbs शायद and संभव both mean 'perhaps, maybe' *only* when used with the subjunctive; they mean 'probably' when the subjunctive is not used:

वह शायद आए ।	He may perhaps come.
वह शायद नहीं आएगा ।	He probably will not come.

The imperfect, continuous, and perfect tenses all have subjunctive forms in which the subjunctive of होना is used as the auxiliary:

गीता यहाँ रहती हो ।	Geeta may live here.
दिनकर अकेला जा रहा हो ।	Dinkar may be going alone.
वह दफ़्तर गया हो ।	He may have gone to the office.

Perfect Tenses

The perfect tenses describe completed actions. Verb forms in these tenses are built using the perfect participle. The perfect participle of a verb is formed by adding आ, ई, ए, or ई to the verb stem. For example, the perfect participle of हँसना is हँसा (masc. sing.), हँसी (fem. sing.), हँसे (masc. pl.), and हँसी (fem. pl.). Verbs whose stems end in आ, ओ, ए, or ई add य to the stem in the masculine singular form (e.g., the perfect participle of आना is आया in the masculine singular). Verbs whose stems end in ऊ or ई have these vowels shortened to उ or इ in the perfect participle (e.g., the perfect participle of छूना 'to touch,' is छुआ in the masculine singular).

In the perfect tenses, न or नहीं is used to negate the verb.

Intransitive Verbs

Intransitive verbs are verbs which do not take a direct object, such as जाना 'to go,' आना 'to come,' हँसना 'to laugh,' मरना 'to die,' उठना 'to rise,' and बैठना 'to sit.' Intransitive verbs agree with their subject in the perfect tenses.

PERFECT

मैं हँसा/ हँसी	I laughed
तू हँसा/ हँसी	you laughed
वह हँसा/ हँसी	he/she laughed
हम हँसे/ हँसीं	we laughed
तुम हँसे/ हँसीं	you laughed
आप हँसे / हँसीं	you laughed
वे हँसे / हँसीं	they laughed

PRESENT PERFECT

मैं हँसा हूँ / हँसी हूँ	I have laughed
तू हँसा है / हँसी है	you have laughed
वह हँसा है / हँसी है	he/she has laughed
हम हँसे हैं/ हँसी हैं	we have laughed
तुम हँसे हो / हँसी हो	you have laughed
आप हँसे हैं / हँसी हैं	you have laughed
वे हँसे हैं / हँसी हैं	they have laughed

PAST PERFECT

मैं हँसा था / हँसी थी	I had laughed
तू हँसा था / हँसी थी	you had laughed
वह हँसा था / हँसी थी	he/she had laughed
हम हँसे थे / हँसी थीं	we had laughed
तुम हँसे थे / हँसी थीं	you had laughed
आप हँसे थे / हँसी थीं	you had laughed
वे हँसे थे / हँसी थीं	they had laughed

FUTURE PERFECT

This tense is used to describe actions that will be completed in the future and to make assumptions about past events.

मैं हँसा हूँगा / हँसी हूँगी	I will/must have laughed
तू हँसा होगा / हँसी होगी	you will/must have laughed
वह हँसा होगा / हँसी होगी	he/she will/must have laughed
हम हँसे होंगे / हँसी होंगी	we will/must have laughed
तुम हँसे होगे / हँसी होगी	you will/must have laughed
आप हँसे होंगे / हँसी होंगी	you will/must have laughed
वे हँसे होंगे / हँसी होंगी	they will/must have laughed

THE IRREGULAR PERFECT PARTICIPLES OF जाना (TO GO)

मैं गया / गई	I went
तू गया / गई	you went
वह गया / गई	he/she went
हम गए / गई	we went
तुम गए / गई	you went
आप गए / गई	you went
वे गए / गई	they went

Transitive Verbs

Transitive verbs are verbs which take a direct object, such as देखना 'to see,' करना 'to do,' and बनाना 'to make.' A general rule of thumb for determining whether or not a verb is transitive is, If you can ask *what?* of the verb, then it is most likely transitive (e.g., *What* do you see? *What* do you do?).

In the perfect tenses transitive verbs agree in gender and number with their direct object, and the 'logical subject' (i.e., that which would be the subject in an equivalent English sentence) takes the postposition ने:[3]

> लड़की ने कमरा देखा ।   The girl saw the room.

In this sentence, देखा agrees with the direct object कमरा, and the logical subject लड़की takes ने.

If there is no direct object (either present or implied), or if the direct object of the verb is governed by a postposition, then the verb becomes 'neutral' in form, that is, masculine singular:

> हमने लड़की को कहा...   We said to the girl…

The patterns for transitive verbs in the perfect tenses which are given on the following pages are shown only with the pronoun मैंने since the pronoun has no effect on the form of the verb:

> मैंने कमरा देखा ।   I saw the room.
> आपने कमरा देखा ।   You saw the room. (etc.)

Note: The gender and number of the direct object is indicated in brackets.

---

[3] Pronouns used with ने have the form: मैंने, तूने, उसने, इसने, हमने, तुमने, आपने, उन्होंने, इन्होंने.

PERFECT

मैंने कमरा देखा ।	I saw the room. (masc. sing.)
मैंने मेज़ देखी ।	I saw the table. (fem. sing.)
मैंने कमरे देखे ।	I saw the rooms. (masc. pl.)
मैंने मेज़ें देखीं ।	I saw the tables. (fem. pl.)
मैंने कमरे में देखा ।	I looked in the room. (neutral)

PRESENT PERFECT

मैंने कमरा देखा है ।	I have seen the room. (masc. sing.)
मैंने मेज़ देखी है ।	I have seen the table. (fem. sing.)
मैंने कमरे देखे हैं ।	I have seen the rooms. (masc. pl.)
मैंने मेज़ें देखी हैं ।	I have seen the tables. (fem. pl.)
मैंने कमरे में देखा है ।	I have looked in the room. (neutral)

PAST PERFECT

मैंने कमरा देखा था ।	I had seen the room. (masc. sing.)
मैंने मेज़ देखी थी ।	I had seen the table. (fem. sing.)
मैंने कमरे देखे थे ।	I had seen the rooms. (masc. pl.)
मैंने मेज़ें देखी थीं ।	I had seen the tables. (fem. pl.)
मैंने कमरे में देखा था ।	I had looked in the room. (neutral)

FUTURE PERFECT

This tense is used to describe actions that will be completed in the future and to make assumptions about past events.

मैंने कमरा देखा होगा ।	I will/must have seen the room.
मैंने मेज़ देखी होगी ।	I will/must have seen the table.
मैंने कमरे देखे होंगे ।	I will/must have seen the rooms.
मैंने मेज़ें देखी होंगी ।	I will/must have seen the tables.
मैंने कमरे में देखा होगा ।	I will/must have looked in the room.

TRANSITIVE VERBS WITH IRREGULAR PERFECT PARTICIPLES

	masc. sing.	fem. sing.	masc. pl.	fem. pl.
करना (to do)	किया	की	किए	कीं
पीना (to drink)	पिया	पी	पिए	पीं
लेना (to take)	लिया	ली	लिए	लीं
देना (to give)	दिया	दी	दिए	दीं

Notes:

1. The perfect participles of conjunct verbs formed with करना, in which the first component of the verb is a noun (e.g., काम करना 'to work,' इच्छा करना 'to desire') agree with the noun component of the verb:

मैंने काम किया ।	I worked. (काम is a masculine noun.)
मैंने इच्छा की ।	I desired. (इच्छा is a feminine noun.)

2. The verbs लाना 'to bring' and भूलना 'to forget' are intransitive despite their transitive appearance, and do not take the ने construction.

Verbs with Transitive and Intransitive Uses

There are a few verbs that are usually conjugated as intransitive verbs but which, when a direct object is present or implied, are considered transitive and take the ने construction:

जीतना to win

हारना to lose

बदलना to change

समझना to understand

भरना to fill

क्या वह समझा?	Did he understand? (intransitive)
क्या उसने प्रश्न समझा?	Did he understand the question? (transitive)
बाल्टी पानी से भरी ।	The bucket was filled with water. (intransitive)
मैंने बाल्टी भरी ।	I filled the bucket. (transitive)

The verb बोलना 'to speak' is normally used intransitively, but may be used with ने without any difference in meaning:

मैं उससे बोला ।	I spoke with him/her.
मैंने उससे बोला ।	I spoke with him/her.

The verb पढ़ना 'to read, to study' when meaning 'to read' uses the ने construction. When it means 'to study,' however, it does not use ने:

मैंने किताब पढ़ी ।	I read the book.
लड़का हिन्दी पढ़ा ।	The boy studied Hindi.

116

Verbs Used in Combination

चाहना — When चाहना follows a verb in the infinitive it means 'to want':

मैं देखना चाहता हूँ।	I want to see.
मोहन जाना चाहेगा।	Mohan will want to go.
हमने आना चाहा।	We wanted to come.

When the doer of the desired action is other than the subject, an additional clause linked by कि, is used, in which the verb is in the subjunctive:

| मैं चाहता हूँ कि बसन्त
हिन्दी सीखे। | I want Basant to learn Hindi.
(I want that Basant
should learn Hindi.) |
| वह चाहेगा कि हम आज जाएं। | He will want us to go today. |

सकना — When सकना follows the stem of a verb it means 'to be able to, can.' To make the verb negative, नहीं is placed either before or after the verb stem:

मैं देख सकता हूँ।	I can see.
तुम सुन नहीं सकोगी।	You will not be able to hear.
वे लोग नहीं आ सके।	Those people couldn't come.

The verb सकना is never used alone (i.e., a verb stem must be present). Hence, सकना cannot be used to make the general assertions 'I can,' or 'I cannot.' Note that सकना is intransitive and does not take ने in the perfect tenses.

चुकना — This verb literally means 'to be finished,' but when it follows the stem of a verb it conveys the sense that an action has already been completed:

मैं खा चुका हूँ।	I've already eaten.
वह घर जा चुका था।	He had already gone home.
दो बज चुके हैं।	It's already two o'clock.

117

लगना — When लगना follows the oblique case infinitive[4] of a verb, it means 'to begin to.' This construction is never used in the imperative or continuous tenses:

वह अपना कमरा साफ करने लगा ।[5]	He began cleaning his room.
मैं आपके बारे में सोचने लगा ।	I began thinking about you.
वह शीघ्र दुकान पर काम करने लगेगा ।	He will begin working at the store soon.

देना — When देना follows the oblique case infinitive of a verb, it means 'to allow to' or 'to let':

रहने दो !	Let it be!
वह मुझे जाने देगा ।	He will allow me to go.
उसे अपना काम करने दीजिए !	Let him do his work!

रहना — When रहना (literally 'to remain') follows the imperfect participle of a verb, it conveys the sense that the action continues over a period of time (i.e., it 'keeps on' or 'goes on'):

वह बढ़ता रहता है ।	He keeps on growing.
वे दिन भर काम करते रहते हैं ।	They keep working all day long.
हिन्दी पढ़ते रहो !	Keep studying Hindi!
हम जाते रहेंगे ।	We will keep going.

जाना — The verb जाना is used in the same way with the imperfect participle, especially when the action progresses in stages:

उसके बाल झड़ते जाते हैं ।	His hair keeps falling out.

---

[4] In the oblique case the ना ending of an infinitive becomes ने.

[5] लगना is intransitive and does not use the ने construction in the perfect tenses.

Verbal Constructions Using को

A wide variety of constructions use the postposition को or the objective pronouns. The flavour of these constructions is typified by the following example:

पिता जी को खुशी थी ।   Father was happy.

                                     (To Father happiness was.)

This construction is very frequently used to express that certain feelings, mental and physical states, knowing, liking, need, advice, belief, compulsion, etc. 'come', 'appear', or simply 'are' to someone.

All constructions share these rules:

1. What would be the logical subject in English, in Hindi takes the postposition को or is an objective pronoun (e.g., मुझे, उसे, तुम्हें, etc.).

2. The verb agrees in gender and number with the noun or pronoun – either present or implied – in the direct case (i.e., not followed by a postposition).

3. If no noun or pronoun in the direct case is present or implied, then the verb is masculine singular in form.

In the above example, पिता जी is the logical subject and therefore takes को, and थी agrees with the feminine noun खुशी. Further examples of this type of construction are given in the following pages.

Knowing

A number of constructions are used to express knowledge or knowing. The words most often used in these constructions are: पता (m) 'clue,' मालूम (adj.) 'known,' and जानकारी (f) 'information':

मुझे पता है ।	I know. (To me a clue is.)
हमको मालूम नहीं था ।	We didn't know.
	(To us it wasn't known)[6].
मुझे इस बात की जानकारी थी ।	I knew of this matter.
	(To me information of this matter was.)

In a similar construction the verb आना 'to come,' is used to express possession of an acquired skill or knowledge:

ज्योति को हिन्दी आती है ।	Jyoti knows Hindi.
	(Hindi comes to Jyoti.)
क्या आपको अँग्रेज़ी आती है?	Do you know English?
क्या उसे पढ़ना आता है?	Does he know how to read?

Hoping/Desiring/Believing

These constructions use the nouns आशा (f) 'hope,' इच्छा (f) 'desire,' and विश्वास (m) 'belief':

मुझे आशा है कि ...	I hope that...
	(To me the hope is that...)
उनको आशा है कि वह आएगी ।	They hope that she will come.
सीमा को शरीफ़ पति पाने की इच्छा है ।	Seema desires to find a decent husband.
उसको विश्वास है कि राम झूठ बोल रहा है ।	He/she believes that Raam is lying.

---

[6] Note that मालूम is an adjective and will not influence the verb.

Should/Need to

Two common constructions use the word चाहिए. When चाहिए is preceded by a verb in the infinitive it has the meaning 'should' or 'need to':

मुझे देखना चाहिए ।	I should (need to) see.
उसे बाद में आना चाहिए ।	He/she should come later.
हमको जाना चाहिए था ।	We should have gone.

When the verb has a direct object, the verb and the auxiliary (if present) agree with the direct object:

आपको मेज़ लानी चाहिए ।	You should bring the table.
आपको मेज़ लानी चाहिए थी ।	You should have brought the table.

When चाहिए is preceded by a noun it means 'want' or 'need' and it agrees with the noun:

मुझे चाय चाहिए ।	I want tea.
आपको एक किताब चाहिए थी ।	You needed a book.
दृष्टि को दो सेब चाहिएँ ।	Drishti needs two apples.
हमको कुछ मेज़ें चाहिएँ थीं ।	We wanted some tables.

Have to

This construction implies a sense of compulsion. A verb is used in the infinitive with the auxiliary होना:

मुझे इसको छोड़ना है ।	I have to leave this.
ज्योति पुंज को जाना था ।	Jyoti Punj had to go.
उसे सब्ज़ी खरीदनी होगी ।	He/she will have to buy vegetable(s).

Must

This construction expresses a stronger sense of compulsion. When पड़ना (literally, 'to fall') follows the infinitive of a verb it means 'must' or 'have to':

माता जी को रोज़ खाना बनाना पड़ता है।	Mother must cook food every day.
हमें जाना पड़ा।	We had to go.
मुझे देखना पड़ेगा।	I will have to see.

Liking/Disliking

One construction which expresses like or dislike uses the noun पसन्द (f) 'liking':

हमें टी.वी. देखना पसन्द है।	We like to watch TV. (To us liking to watch TV is.)
रेखा को वह फ़िल्म पसन्द नहीं आएगी।	Raykha will not like that film.

In another construction अच्छा लगना (to seem good) is used. Both the adjective अच्छा and the verb लगना agree with the object that is liked:

लड़के को फल अच्छा लगता है।	The boy likes fruit. (To the boy fruit seems good.)
क्या आपको भारत अच्छा लगा?	Did you like India?
कौन-से देश उसे अच्छे लगते हैं?	Which countries does he like?
मुझे यह तस्वीर अच्छी नहीं लगती।	I don't like this picture.

In the same manner बुरा लगना (to seem bad) can be used to express dislike:

मुझे यह तस्वीर बुरी लगती है।	I don't like this picture.

122

Physical Conditions

Physical states, conditions, or sensations occurring in the human body are almost always expressed using this construction:

मुझे बुखार है ।	I have a fever.
उसको जुकाम था ।	He/she had a cold.
बच्चे को चक्कर आता है ।	The child is dizzy.

The verb most commonly used to express physical conditions is लगना (to be applied). The noun corresponding to the condition (e.g., thirst, hunger, pain, heat, etc.) precedes लगना, and लगना agrees with that noun:

मुझे प्यास लगी है ।	I am thirsty.
	(Thirst has been applied to me.)
हमको भूख लग रही है ।	We are feeling hungry.
तुमको चोट नहीं लगेगी ।	You will not get hurt.
पुष्प को ठंड लग रही है ।	Pushpa is feeling cold.

Mental States

Mental states or conditions are also often expressed using this construction:

कोमलता को बहुत सुख है ।	Komaltaa is very happy.
उसे दुःख होगा ।	He will be unhappy.
आपसे मिलकर मुझे बहुत खुशी हुई ।	I am (literally, 'was') very delighted to meet you.
मुझे अफ़सोस है ।	I am sorry.
बच्चों को डर लगा ।	The children felt afraid.
मुझे शंका है कि वे आएँ ।	I doubt that they will (would) come.

Remembering/Missing

One way of expressing 'to remember' is to use याद होना. The verb agrees with the person or object remembered (if present):

मुझे याद नहीं है ।	I don't remember.
चेतना को मेरा जन्म दिन याद था ।	Chaytna remembered my birthday.
गगन को तुम्हारी कहानी याद हो गई ।	Gagan remembered your story.
जो आपने कहा वह मुझे याद नहीं होगा ।	I will not remember what you said.

To express missing (की) याद आना is used. The verb आना agrees with याद (f) 'memory, recollection' and not with the person or object remembered:

दिनकर को आज-कल अपने पिता-जी की याद आती है ।	Dinkar misses his father these days.

याद आना is also used to mean 'to remember suddenly' or 'to strike one.' However, in this usage याद functions as an adjective and आना agrees with the thing remembered:

प्रेम को अपने भाई का वचन याद आया ।	Praym suddenly remembered his brother's promise.

To Get/Obtain

In this construction मिलना has the meaning 'to get':

मुझे समाचार पत्र मिल रहा है ।	I am getting a newspaper.
क्या आपको चिट्ठी मिली ?	Did you get a letter?
उसको शान्ति मिलेगी ।	He/she will get peace.

मिलना can also mean 'to be available' or 'to be found':

आपको रेल गाड़ी के स्टेशन पर रिक्षा मिलेगा ।	You will find a rickshaw at the train station.
बाज़ार में अच्छी मेज़ें मिलती हैं ।	Good tables are available in the bazaar.
बन्दर इस मन्दिर में हमेशा मिलते हैं ।	Monkeys are always found in this temple.

Passive Voice

In these constructions the passive sense of a verb is shown. In the passive voice, the action expressed by the verb is performed <u>on</u> the subject, whereas in the active voice the action is performed <u>by</u> the subject. For example: 'He sent the letter' (active), and 'The letter was sent by him' (passive).

There are two kinds of passive constructions in Hindi and in both, the perfect participle of a verb (e.g., देखा) is used with the verb जाना.

In the first type of construction, the verb agrees with the subject of the sentence, and the same word will be the subject in both the English and Hindi sentences:

वह देखा गया था ।	It had been seen.
यह कहा जाता था ।	It used to be said.
मेरी किताब ली गई ।	My book was taken.
यहाँ हिन्दी पढ़ाई जा रही है ।	Hindi is being taught here.
कपड़े धोए होंगे ।	The clothes will be washed.
सेब उसको दिए गए हैं ।	Apples have been given to him.

In the second kind of passive construction, what would be, in English, the logical subject takes the postposition को or is an objective pronoun, and both the perfect participle and the verb जाना are in the masculine singular form:

मुझे बताया जाता है ।	I am told. (It is told to me.)
आज एक गीत को पढ़ाया जाएगा ।	A song will be taught today.
हमको बताया जा रहा था ।	We were being told.
गेंद को पकड़ा गया ।	The ball was caught.

If an agent is mentioned (i.e., the one who performs the action), then the agent will be followed by the postpositions के द्वारा or से:

मेरा मकान हंस राज के द्वारा बनाया गया था ।	My house had been built by Hans Raaj.
खाना माता-जी से भेजा जाएगा ।	The food will be sent by Mother.
हिन्दी भाषा को चीनी लोगों से नहीं बोला जाता ।	Hindi is not spoken by Chinese people.

The Suffix कर

The suffix कर added to a verb stem has the meaning 'after having done.' An English sentence such as 'I looked and laughed,' in which two verbs joined by 'and' have the same subject, is often rendered in Hindi as a sentence in which the first of the two verbs takes the suffix कर, giving a sentence of the form 'Having looked, I laughed.' In informal speech, the suffix के can be used instead of कर. The verb करना, however, always uses the के form of this suffix (i.e., करके):

मैं बाज़ार जाकर एक किताब खरीदूँगा ।	I will go to town and buy a book.
मैंने खाना खाकर अपनी किताब पढ़ी ।	After eating food I read my book.
वह काम खत्म करके यहाँ आया ।	He finished work and came here.

This verb form can also be used as an adverb:

वह दौड़कर आया ।	He came running.
मैं सोचकर काम करता हूँ ।	I work thoughtfully (carefully).

127

Uses of the Oblique Infinitive

Verbs can also be used with postpositions. When a postposition follows a verb, the verb must be in the oblique form:[7]

नहाने के बाद् यहाँ आइए ।   Come here <u>after bathing</u>.

दिल्ली पहुँचने पर मैंने   <u>Upon reaching</u> Delhi I
आराम किया ।   rested.

मैं हिन्दी सीखने के लिए   I went to India to learn
भारत गया ।   (<u>for learning</u>) Hindi.

हम खाना खाने को तैयार हैं ।   We are ready <u>to eat</u> food.

To indicate purpose, as in the previous two examples, the oblique infinitive may be used without a postposition:

मैं हिन्दी <u>सीखने</u> भारत गयां ।   I went to India <u>to learn</u> Hindi.

Possessive pronouns may also be used with the oblique case infinitive:

<u>मेरे आने से पहले</u> वह गया ।   He went before I came.
                                          (<u>Before my coming</u>, he
                                          went.)

बच्चों के जाने के बाद्   Rest after the children
आराम कीजिए ।   go. (<u>After the children's
                                          going</u>, rest.)

मेरे जाने में कोई फ़ायदा   There isn't any point <u>in my
नहीं है ।   going</u>.

With the possessive postposition, the oblique infinitive modifies a noun:

पीने का पानी   drinking water
जाने का समय   departure time
रोने की बात   something to cry about (crying matter)

---

[7] Recall that in the oblique case the ना ending of an infinitive becomes ने.

Verbal Expressions Whose Objects Take का, की, के

Many verbal expressions require their objects to be followed by particular postpositions. Some verbal expressions formed with करना 'to do' (e.g., इन्तज़ार करना 'to wait,' मदद करना 'to help') require their objects to take a possessive postposition (usually का or की).

Observe that the first component of these verbal expressions is a noun. इन्तज़ार is a masculine noun meaning 'the act of waiting,' and मदद is a feminine noun meaning 'help.' When these expressions are used, the logical object (e.g., आदमी in the Hindi sentence below) 'possesses' the noun component (इन्तज़ार), and the possessive postposition agrees with the noun component, rather than the logical object:

मैं आदमी का इन्तज़ार   I wait for the man. (I do the
करता हूँ ।   waiting of the man.)

If the logical object of the verb is a pronoun, its possessive form is used:

मेरी मदद कीजिए !   Help me! (Do my help.)

In the perfect tenses, the perfect participle of करना agrees with the noun component of the verbal expression:

आपने किताब की तलाश की ।   You looked for the book.
                             (You did the search of the
                             book.)

In the above sentence, the feminine perfect participle of करना (की) agrees with तलाश, a feminine noun meaning 'search.'

Compound Verbs

Compound verbs are used frequently in Hindi. Verbs of this type consist of a verb stem (the *main* verb) combined with an auxiliary verb to form a single compound verb:

बैठ जाना to sit down

The meaning of the compound verb is *similar* to that of the main verb; the auxiliary verb colours or influences the meaning of the main verb in some way. For example, the main verb of the compound verb बैठ जाना is बैठना 'to sit.' When the auxiliary जाना is added, the meaning becomes 'to sit down,' and जाना no longer conveys its usual meaning (i.e., 'to go'):

वह सीढ़ियों पर बैठ गया ।   He sat down on the stairs.

Compound verbs share these characteristics:

1.   Compound verbs are seldom used in the continuous tenses.

2.   Compound verbs are not normally used in the negative:

मैंने भोजन ले लिया ।   I took food.[8]

but मैंने भोजन नहीं लिया ।   I didn't take food.

3.   Only when both the main verb and the auxiliary are transitive is the compound verb transitive, thus taking the ने construction in the perfect tenses:

मैंने भोजन खा लिया ।   I ate food.

Since both खाना 'to eat' and लेना 'to take' are transitive, खा लेना is transitive.

The verbs most often found as auxiliaries in compound verbs and the manner in which they influence the meaning of the main verb are described next.

---

[8] In Hindi, a common way of saying 'I ate' is to say, 'I took food.'

जाना

जाना is perhaps the most widely used auxiliary in compound verbs. The presence of जाना may convey the sense that the action of the main verb is (in some way) finished or complete:

खाना	to eat	खा जाना	to eat (it all)
पीना	to drink	पी जाना	to drink (it all)
पढ़ना	to read	पढ़ जाना	to read (it all)
मरना	to die	मर जाना	to die

The presence of जाना may also suggest that the action is done in stages, progressively, or as a process:

सोना	to sleep	सो जाना	to go to sleep
आना	to come	आ जाना	to keep coming
होना	to be	हो जाना	to become
भूलना	to forget	भूल जाना	to forget

हम ठीक समय पर पहुँच जाएंगे ।	We will arrive at the right time.
दुर्घटना में तीन आदमी मर गए ।	Three men died in the accident.
वह प्रतिदिन बाज़ार आ जाता है ।	He comes to the bazaar every day.
क्या आप अपना चश्मा भूल गए?	Did you forget your glasses?

Compound verbs using जाना are intransitive and do not use the ने construction in the perfect tenses:

| चूहा पनीर खा गया । | The mouse ate (up) the cheese. |

लेना

लेना (literally, 'to take') as an auxiliary verb can convey the sense that the action is primarily of interest to the doer of the action, or that the action is in some way directed towards the doer. It also may suggest that the action is done with effort:

रमेश अपना काम कर लेता है ।	Ramaysh does his work.
देख लीजिए !	Take a look! (for yourself)
बच्चों ने गेंद पकड़ ली ।	The children (just managed to catch) caught the ball.

देना

देना (literally, 'to give') as an auxiliary verb conveys the sense that the action is primarily of interest to someone other than the doer of the action, or that the action is performed for someone else. It may also suggest that the action is in some way directed away from the doer:

मैं आपका काम खत्म कर दूँगा ।	I will finish your work.
मेरे लिए यह काम कर दो ।	Do this work for me.
किसने किताब वहाँ रख दी ?	Who put the book (over) there?

डालना

डालना (literally, 'to throw down' or 'to pour') implies that the action is done with aggression or vehemence:

उसने पागल कुत्ते को मार डाला ।	He killed the rabid dog.
मैंने शीशा तोड़ डाला ।	I broke the mirror.

निकलना

निकलना (literally, 'to emerge') as an auxiliary with verbs of motion suggests that the action is done suddenly or in an unexpected fashion. Sometimes its original meaning is lent to the main verb:

बिल्ली खिड़की से अचानक आ निकली ।	The cat suddenly came out of the window.
बादलों में से चन्द्रमा आ निकला ।	The moon (suddenly) emerged from behind the clouds.

उठना

उठना (literally, 'to arise') may imply suddenness or indicate that the action is moving or directed upwards:

हम हँस उठे ।	We burst out laughing.
वह सीढ़ियों से ऊपर भाग उठा ।	He ran up the stairs.

पड़ना

पड़ना (literally, 'to fall') also implies a sense of suddenness but may suggest that the action is moving or directed downwards:

मेरे हाथों से सारी किताबें गिर पड़ीं ।	All the books fell (suddenly) from my hands.
राम रो पड़ा ।	Raam burst out crying.
बिल्ली दीवार से कूद पड़ी ।	The cat jumped off the wall.

Verbs Whose Objects Require से

Some verbs require the use of the postposition से with their object, most notably कहना 'to say,' पूछना 'to ask,' बात करना 'to talk,' माँगना 'to request,' and मिलना 'to meet.'[9] The meaning of से varies according to the verb:

हम अपने अध्यापक से आज मिलेंगे ।	We will meet (with) our teacher today.
मैंने लड़के से नमस्ते कहा ।	I said hello to the boy.
दिनकर हिन्दी में चेतना से बात करता है ।	Dinkar talks in Hindi to Chaytna.
मैं गुरु-जी से एक प्रश्न पूछूँगा ।	I will ask (from) Guru-jee one question.
श्याम लड़के से दो सेब माँग रहा है ।	Shyam is requesting two apples from the boy.

The Verbs बैठना, खड़ा होना, and लेटना

The verbs बैठना 'to sit,' खड़ा होना 'to stand,' and लेटना 'to lie down,' represent continued action (as in, 'I sat and am still sitting') and are exceptions, using the imperfect tenses instead of the continuous tenses:

मैं बैठा हूँ । not मैं बैठ रहा हूँ ।	I am sitting.
मैं बैठा था । not मैं बैठ रहा था ।	I was sitting.

---

[9] When मिलना is used to describe intentional meeting, its object takes से; when the meeting is by chance or is unplanned, the object takes को (e.g., हम सड़क पर दादा-जी को मिले । We ran into Dada-jee on the road).

हम बाहर खड़े हैं ।	We are standing outside.
वह बारिश में खड़ी थी ।	She was standing in the rain.
चेतना का कुत्ता पलंग पर लेटा है ।	Chaytna's dog is lying on the bed.

Additional uses of पड़ना

The use of पड़ना to express 'must' (see pg. 122) and as an auxiliary verb in compound verbs (see pg. 133) has already been described. Two other usages of पड़ना are given below:

To fall:

बिहार में मुसीबत पड़ी ।	Misfortune fell on Bihaar.
इस वर्ष मेरा जन्म-दिन सोमवार को पड़ता है ।	This year my birthday falls on Monday.
बारिश पड़ रही है ।	It's raining. (Rain is falling.)
राजस्थान में सूखा पड़ा ।	There's a drought (drought fell) in Rajasthan.

To lie (for inanimate objects):

किताब मेज़ पर पड़ी है ।	The book is lying on the table.
आपका घर मेरे रास्ते में पड़ता है ।	Your house lies on my way.
मकान खाली पड़ा है ।	The house is lying vacant.

Additional Uses of लगना

लगना, an extremely versatile verb, is heard very frequently and is used in a wide variety of contexts in addition to those already described earlier in this chapter (see pages 118 and 122). The most common of its meanings are presented below:

To be applied/attached to:

पंखा छत पर लगा है ।	The fan is attached to the ceiling.
सफ़ेद कपड़े पर रँग लगा है ।	The white cloth got stained. (Colour has been applied to the white cloth.)

To suit:

राम पर लाल वाले कपड़े अच्छे नहीं लगते ।	Red (coloured) clothes do not suit Raam.
यह टोपी आप पर अच्छी लगती है ।	This hat suits you well.

To resemble or to be related:

वह अपने भाई जैसा लगता है ।	He looks like his brother.
वह बुढ़िया-सी लगती थी ।	She used to look like an old woman.

To fit:

शीशा दरवाज़े में नहीं लगेगा ।	The glass will not fit the door.

To appear/seem, to strike:

लगता है कि बहुत लोग यहाँ नहीं आते ।	It appears that many people don't come here.
ऐसा लगा कि बारिश आएगी ।	It seemed that the rain would come.
उसको कठिन लगा ।	It seemed difficult to him.
आपको कैसा लगता है ?	How does it strike you?
मुझे लगता है कि आजकल संतरे और महँगे होते हैं ।	It seems to me that oranges are more expensive these days.

A common way of describing the qualities of a person is to use लगना with the subject in the direct case:

आप सुन्दर लगते हैं ।	You are beautiful. (You seem to be beautiful.)
वह समझदार लगता है ।	He seems intelligent.

To take time to do something:

In this construction, the action which requires time is represented by an oblique case infinitive with the postposition में 'in' (e.g., बनाने में 'in making,' जाने में 'in going'):

इस दुकान को बनाने में, दो साल लगे ।	It took two years to build this store.
कितना समय लगेगा ?	How much time will it take?
पाँच ही मिनट लगेंगे ।	It will take only five minutes.
दिल्ली जाने में कितनी देर लगेगी ?	How long will it take to go to Delhi?
दिल्ली पहुँचने में सात घंटे लगते हैं ।	It takes seven hours to reach Delhi.

Constructions with Participles

Adjectival Uses

Both imperfect and perfect participles can be used adjectivally. Used as an adjective, a participle agrees in number and gender with the noun it describes.

Imperfect participles (e.g., देखता 'seeing,' चलता 'moving,' हँसता 'laughing') attribute an action in progress to their noun:

हँसता आदमी	laughing man
चलती गाड़ी	moving vehicle
खिलते फूल	blossoming flowers

Imperfect participles are sometimes followed by the participle हुआ, हुई, or हुए, which also agrees with the noun it describes:

चलता हुआ पंखा	moving fan
चलती हुई गाड़ी	moving vehicle
खिलते हुए फूल	blossoming flowers

बहता पानी साफ होता है ।	Flowing water is clean.
चलती गाड़ी पर मत चढ़ो ।	Do not board a moving vehicle.
खिलते हुए फूलों को मत तोड़ो !	Don't pluck the blossoming flowers!

Perfect participles (e.g., देखा 'seen,' लिखा 'written,' खरीदा 'bought') are similarly used as adjectives but are always followed by हुआ, हुई, or हुए. Perfect participles associate a completed action with their noun:

खरीदा हुआ कपड़ा	bought cloth
लिखी हुई किताब	written book
जले हुए वृक्ष	burnt trees

दिल्ली से खरीदा हुआ कपड़ा मुझे पसन्द है ।	I like the cloth bought in Delhi.
मैंने भक्ति नाथ की लिखी हुई किताब पढ़ी है ।	I have read the book written by Bhakti Naath.
हमने जले हुए वृक्ष देखे ।	We saw the burnt trees.

Adverbial Uses

The imperfect participle is used in a number of adverbial constructions, always with the ए ending (e.g., देखते, करते, etc.).

To express the sense 'while doing,' or two actions going on at the same time, the imperfect participle is followed by हुए:

करते हुए	while doing
देखते हुए	while seeing

औरत काम करते हुए गा रही थी ।	The woman was singing while working.
ज्ञान हँसते हुए बोली कि...	Gyaan laughingly said that....
मैंने श्याम को जाते हुए देखा ।	I saw Shyam while (he was) going.
हमने आदमी को आते हुए देखा ।	We saw the man coming.
कान्ति ने आपको गाते हुए सुना ।	Kaanti heard you singing.

The position of the participle in the sentence determines the verb it is modifying. Compare the following:

मैंने खाते हुए आपको देखा ।	I saw you while (I was) eating.
मैंने आपको खाते हुए देखा ।	I saw you while (you were) eating.

Another way of expressing 'while' is to follow the imperfect participle with the noun समय 'time':

लौटते समय मैं गिर गया ।	I fell while (at the time of) returning.
वह पानी बरसते समय बाहर नहीं जा सकता ।	He can't go outside while it is raining.

Repetition of the imperfect participle (without हुए) suggests that the action is repetitive or continuous:

मैं हिन्दी सुनते सुनते सीखूँगा ।	Hearing (again and again) I will learn Hindi.
वह चलते चलते शिखर पर पहुँचा ।	(Step by step, gradually) he reached the summit.
मैं दौड़ते दौड़ते थक गया ।	Running and running, I got tired.
वह पढ़ते पढ़ते सो गई ।	She fell asleep reading.

When the imperfect participle is followed by ही, it has the meaning 'as soon as':

वह चुटकुला सुनते ही हँस पड़ी ।	As soon as she heard the joke, she burst out laughing.
वहाँ पहुँचते ही हम खाना खाएंगे ।	We will eat as soon as we arrive there.

Verbs with Related Stems

There are many groups of verbs whose spellings closely resemble each other and whose meanings are related. A frequently encountered pair of this type is made up of an intransitive verb and its transitive counterpart; for example, the intransitive verb मरना 'to die' and its transitive counterpart मारना 'to kill.' Such pairs are usually fairly easy to identify and often involve the lengthening of a vowel in the stem of the intransitive verb:

INTRANSITIVE		TRANSITIVE	
उतरना	to get down	उतारना	to take down
पहुँचना	to arrive	पहुँचाना	to deliver
ठहरना	to stay	ठहराना	to stop
बैठना	to sit	बैठाना	to seat
मिलना	to meet	मिलाना	to introduce
उठना	to get up	उठाना	to raise, lift
सोना	to sleep	सुलाना	to put to sleep

Some pairs of transitive verbs are also similarly related:

TRANSITIVE		TRANSITIVE	
देखना	to see	दिखाना	to show
करना	to do	कराना	to get done
खाना	to eat	खिलाना	to feed
पीना	to drink	पिलाना	to give a drink

The so-called causative verbs (whose stems end in वा) convey the sense that an action is made (caused) to happen or take place (e.g., बनवाना 'to get made'). The actual doer of the action, if specified, takes the postposition से:

गुरु-जी ने अध्यापक से छात्र को बुलवाया ।	The master had the teacher call the student.
इन्द्रा ने राम से शिव को जगवाया ।	Indra had Raam wake up Shiv.

Causative verbs are all related to groups of verbs like those shown above:

INTRANSITIVE OR TRANSITIVE		TRANSITIVE		CAUSATIVE	
चलना	to move	चलाना	to drive	चलवाना	to get moved
बनना	to become	बनाना	to make	बनवाना	to get made
सुनना	to hear	सुनाना	to relate, tell	सुनवाना	to get told
देखना	to see	दिखाना	to show	दिखवाना	to get shown
करना	to do	कराना	to get done	करवाना	to get done
खाना	to eat	खिलाना	to feed	खिलवाना	to get fed
बोलना	to speak	बुलाना	to call	बुलवाना	to get called

मैंने यह बात सुनी है ।	I've heard of this matter (thing).
मैंने उसको यह बात सुनाई ।	I told him of this matter.
मैंने यह बात अपने मित्र से उसको सुनवाई ।	I had my friend tell him of this matter.

यह मकान पिछले साल बना था ।	This house was built last year.
उसने पिछले साल अपना मकान बनाया ।	He built his house last year.
उसने पिछले साल अपना मकान बनवाया ।	He had his house built last year.
मोटर गाड़ी ठीक नहीं चलती ।	The car doesn't run well.
मोहन मोटर गाड़ी नहीं चलाता ।	Mohan doesn't drive a car.
राज अपने मित्र से मोटर गाड़ी चलवाता है ।	Raaj gets his friend to drive the car.

A

abandon - (का) त्याग करना,
 छोड़ देना

able (be ~) - सकना (see pg. 117)

abuse - गाली देना

accept - मानना, स्वीकार करना

accompany - (का) साथ देना

accuse - आरोप लगाना

adjust - ठीक-ठाक करना

advance - बढ़ना

advise - सलाह देना

affect (influence) - असर पड़ना

agree - (से) सहमत होना

announce - एलान करना

answer - उत्तर देना

apologize - क्षमा करना,
 माफ़ करना

appear (seem) - दिखना

apply - लगाना

appoint - लगाना

appreciate - (की) प्रशंसा करना

approve - स्वीकृति देना,
 मंजूरी देना

argue - तर्क करना

arrange (things) - सजाना

arrest - गिरफ़्तार करना

arrive - पहुँचना

ascertain - यकीन करना

ask - (से) पूछना

assemble - एकत्रित करना

assure - विश्वास दिलाना,
 पक्का करना

attach - लगाना

attack - (पर) आक्रमण करना,
 (पर) हमला करना

attend (presence) -
 उपस्थित होना, हाज़िर होना

attend (with the mind) -
 (पर) ध्यान लगाना

B

babble - बकवास करना

bake - भूनना

bargain - मोलतोल करना

bark - भौंकना

bathe - स्नान करना, नहाना

be - होना

beat - मारना

beaten (be ~) - पिटना

become - हो जाना

beg - भीख माँगना

beg pardon -
 (से) क्षमा माँगना

begin - शुरु करना, आरम्भ
 करना, प्रारम्भ करना

behave - व्यवहार करना

believe - विश्वास करना

belong - (से), संबंधित होना

bend - झुकना

bind - (से) बाँधना

birth (give) - पैदा करना

bite - काटना

blame - (पर) दोष लगाना,
(की) निंदा करना

bleed - खून बहना

blend - मिश्रण करना

bless - आशीर्वाद देना

blink - आँख झपकाना

bloom (flower) - खिलना

blow - फूँकना

boil - उबालना

bore - ऊबा देना

bored (be ~) - ऊबना

born (be ~) - पैदा होना,
जन्म लेना

borrow - उधार माँगना,
उधार लेना

bother - तँग करना,
तकलीफ़ देना

bounce - उछालना

bound (be~) - बँधना

bow - (को) प्रणाम करना

bow (down) - झुकना

break - (को) तोड़ना

break into - घुसना

brighten (up) - निखरना

bring - लाना

broken (be~) - टूटना

build - बनाना

burn - जलना

burn (set fire to) - जलाना

burst - फटना, फूटना

bury - दफ़नाना

buy - खरीदना, मोल लेना

C

calculate - गिनना,
हिसाब लगाना

call - बुलाना, पुकारना

called (be ~) - कहलाना

capture - पकड़ लेना,
बन्दी बनाना,
गिरफ़्तार करना

care (take ~ of) -
(की) परवाह करना,
(की) देखभाल करना

carry - ले जाना

catch - पकड़ना

celebrate - मनाना

certain (be ~) -
(का) यकीन होना

challenge - (को) ललकारना,
(को) चुनौती देना

change - बदलना

charm - रिझाना

chase - (के) पीछे भागना

cheat - धोखा देना

chew - चबाना

choose - चुनना

chop - काटना,
    टुकड़े-टुकड़े करना

clash - (से) टकराना

clean - साफ़ करना

climb - चढ़ना, ऊपर जाना

close - बन्द करना

close eyes - मूँदना

coax - पुचकारना

collect - इकट्ठा करना,
    एकत्रित करना

color - रंग करना

combine, connect - मिलाना

come - आना

come to know - पता चलना

commotion (make ~) -
    लबली मचाना

compassionate (be ~) -
    करुणा होना

compel - विवश करना

compete - (से) मुकाबला करना

complain -
    (की) शिकायत करना

complete - पूरा करना

complicate - उलझाना

condemn - (की) निंदा करना

confront - (से) मुकाबला करना

confused (get ~) -
    उलझन में पड़ना,
    दुविधा में पड़ना

congratulate - बधाई देना

contain - रखना

continue - ज़ारी रखना,
    बना रहना, आगे चलना

control - वश में करना

converse - (से) बात करना

cook - (खाना) बनाना, पकाना

copy - नक़ल करना

correct - ठीक करना

correspond -
    (से) पत्र व्यवहार करना

count - गिनना

cover - ढकना

crackle - चड़चड़ाना

cradle - झूलना

crawl - रेंगना, सरकना

create - (की) रचना करना

creep - रेंगना

criticize -
    (की) आलोचना करना

cross - पार करना

crush - कुचलना

cry - रोना

cure - (का) इलाज करना,
    (की) दवा करना

curse - शाप देना

cut - काटना

cut (be~) - कटना

D

damage - (की) हानि करना, नुक्सान करना

dance - नाचना

deal with - निपटना

debate - (से) बहस करना, वाद-विवाद करना

decay - क्षय होना

decide - निश्चय करना

declare - एलान करना

decorate - सजाना

decrease - कम करना

dedicate - समर्पण करना

defend - (की) रक्षा करना

delay - देर लगाना

deliver - पहुँचाना

deny - नकारना

depart - बिदा होना

depend - (पर) भरोसा करना

deposit - जमा करना

describe - (का) वर्णन करना

desire for - (की) इच्छा करना, तरसना

destroy - मिटाना, संहार करना

detach - (से) अलग करना

develop - (का) विकास करना

diagnose - रोग को पहचानना

die - मरना, मर जाना

dig - खोदना

dig up - उखाड़ना

digest - हज़म करना, पचाना

diminish - घटाना

dine - (का) भोजन करना

dirty - गन्दा करना

disappear - लुप्त हो जाना, गायब होना

disappoint - निराश करना

disappointed (be ~) - निराश होना

discuss - चर्चा करना

disguise - भेष बदलना

dishonor - (का) अपमान करना

disinterested (be ~) - (की) उपेक्षा करना, (में) अरुचि रखना

dislike - (को) नापसन्द करना

dismount - (से) उतरना

dispatch - बिदा करना

dispel - (से) दूर करना

display - प्रदर्शित करना, दिखाना

dissolve - घुलना, घोलना

distribute - बाँटना

disturb - (को) अशान्त करना,
(को) परेशान करना

disturb (things) - (को) छेड़ना

divorce - तलाक देना,
तलाक लेना

do - करना

donate - दान में देना, दान
करना, प्रदान करना

done (get ~) - करवाना

double - दुगना हो जाना

dream - सपना देखना,
स्वप्न देखना

drenched (get ~) - भीगना

drink - पीना

drink (give a ~) -
(को) पिलाना

drip - बूँद-बूँद करके गिरना,
टपकना

drive - चलाना

drop - गिराना

drown - डूबना

dry - सूखना

dust - झाड़ना

dwell - बसना

dye - रंगना

E

earn - कमाना

eat - खाना

echo - प्रतिध्वनि होना, गूँजना

edit - (का) संपादन करना

effect (influence) -
(पर) असर पड़ना

elbow - (को) कोहनी मारना

elect - (का) चुनाव करना

embarrass -
उलझन में डाल देना

embrace - गले लेना

emerge - (से) निकलना

emphasize - (पर) बल देना

endure - बरदास्त करना, सहना

enjoy - आनन्द लेना,
मौज करना, मज़ा आना,
मज़ा लेना

entangle - उलझना

enter - प्रवेश करना

entice - रिझाना

envy - (से) ईर्ष्या करना

erase - मिटाना

erect - सीधा करना,
खड़ा करना

escape - बचना, भाग निकलना

establish - स्थापित करना

evacuate - निकाल ले जाना,
निकाल लाना, ख़ाली करना

evaporate - वाष्पित करना,
भाप बनकर उड़ जाना

evolve - विकसित करना

exaggerate -
  बढ़ा-चढ़ा कर कहना

examine - परखना

exchange - आदान-प्रदान करना

excite - उत्तेजित करना

exclude - अलग करना,
  शामिल न करना

excuse - क्षमा करना

exercise - व्यायाम करना,
  कसरत करना

expand - फैलाना,
  विस्तार करना

expect - आशा करना,
  आशा रखना, उम्मीद करना,
  उम्मीद रखना

experience -
  (का) अनुभव करना

explain - समझाना

explode - विस्फोट करना

explore - छान-बीन करना,
  पता लगाना

export - बाहर भेजना

expose - खुला रखना,
  खुला छोड़ना

express - प्रकट करना,
  अभिव्यक्त करना

extend - फैलाना, लंबा करना,
  पसारना

extinguish - बुझाना

extinguished (be ~) - बुझना

extract - निकालना

F

face - (का) मुकाबला करना,
  (का) सामना करना

fade - मुरझाना

faint - बेहोश होना,
  मूर्च्छित होना

fall - गिरना

fall (out) - झड़ना

fall prey to - (का) शिकार होना

farewell (bid ~) - विदाई देना

favor (do a ~) -
  (का) उपकार करना

fear - डरना

fed up (be ~) - तंग आना

feed - खिलाना

feel - महसूस करना

feel, experience -
  अनुभव करना

fiddle with (touch) - छेड़ना

fight - लड़ना, झगड़ना

fill - भरना

fill up - भर देना

find - पाना

find (time) - समय निकालना,
  फुरसत निकालना

finish - समाप्त करना,
  खत्म करना

fix - ठीक करना

flatter - (की) चापलूसी करना

flee - भागना, भाग जाना

flow - बहना

fly - उड़ना

follow - (के) पीछे चलना,
    (के) पीछे जाना

fool - बेवकूफ़ बनाना,
    बुद्धू बनाना

fooled (be ~) - बेवकूफ़ बनना,
    बुद्धू बनना

forbid - मना करना,
    निषेध करना

force - मज़बूर करना,
    विवश करना

force (apply ~) -
    (पर) ज़ोर लगाना

forget - (को) भूल जाना,
    (को) भूलना

forgive - (को) क्षमा करना,
    (को) माफ़ करना

freeze - जमना

frown - भौंहें चढ़ाना

fry - तलना, पकाना

G

gamble - जुआ खेलना

gather - इकट्ठा करना,
    जमा करना

get - मिलना, प्राप्त करना

get up - उठना

giggle - ही-ही करना

give - देना

give back - वापस देना

glitter - जगमगाना

glue - चिक्कना

go - जाना

go (move) - चलना

gossip - गपशप करना,
    गपशप मारना

grab - पकड़ना, छीनना

grasp (mentally) - ग्रहण करना,
    समझना

graze - चरना

grind - कूटना, पीसना

grow (crops) - उपजना

grow (plants) - उगना

grow up - बढ़ना

growl - गुर्राना

grunt - घुरघुराना

guard - पहरा देना

guess - अनुमान करना

guide - मार्गदर्शन करना,
    मार्गदर्शन लगाना

H

handle - हाथ से पकड़ना

happen - हो जाना

hate - (से) नफ़रत करना

have - के पास

(see Postpositions pg. 89)

heal - (को) स्वस्थ करना

hear - (को) सुनना

heard (be~) - सुनाई देना

heat - गरम करना

help - मदद देना, सहायता देना (की) सहायता करना,

help out - हाथ लगाना

hesitate - संकोच करना, हिचकना

hide (something) - छिपाना

hide (yourself) - छिपना

hike - लम्बी सैर करना

hint - संकेत करना

hold - पकड़ना, रखना

hold on - डटना

hum - गुनगुनाना, गुनगुन करना

humiliate - (को) नीचा दिखाना

hungry (be ~) - भूख लगना

hunt - शिकार करना

hurry - जल्दी करना

hurt (be ~) - चोट लगना

hush - चुप कराना

I

ignore - ध्यान न देना

illuminate - प्रकाशित करना

imagine - कल्पना करना

imitate - नकल करना

immerse - डालना, डुबाना

import - आयात करना

impress - प्रभावित करना

impressed (be ~) - प्रभावित होना

imprint - अंकित करना

imprison - कैद करना, बन्द कर देना

improve - उन्नति करना, सुधारना

inaugurate - (का) उद्घाटन करना

incline (bow down) - झुकना

include - (को) शामिल करना

increase - बढ़ना

indicate - (को) सूचित करना, (पर) इशारा करना

infect - रोग लगाना

infiltrate - घुसना

inform - बताना, सूचित करना, प्रदर्शित करना

informed (be ~) - सूचित होना

inhabit - बसना, निवास करना

inherit - विरासत में पाना

initiate - दीक्षित करना

inject - (से) सुई लगाना

inquire - पूछ-ताछ करना

insist - आग्रह करना

inspire - प्रेरणा देना

inspired (be ~) - प्रेरित होना

install - लगाना

insult - (का) अपमान करना,
  (की) बेइज़्ज़ती करना

insure - (का) बीमा करना

intend - (का) इरादा करना

interfere - (में) हस्तक्षेप करना

introduce - (को) परिचय देना

intrude - घुसना

invent - ईज़ाद करना,
  (का) आविष्कार करना,

investigate - पूछ-ताछ करना,
  जाँच-पड़ताल करना

invite - निमन्त्रण देना, बुलाना

irritate - तंग करना

irritated (be ~) - तंग आना

itch - खुजलाना

J

jealous (be ~) - (से) ईर्ष्या करना

join - जोड़ना

judge - न्याय करना,
  इन्साफ करना

jump - कूदना

K

keep - रखना

kick - (को) लात मारना

kidnap - (का) अपहरण करना

kill - मारना

kiss - चूमना, चुम्बन लेना

knead - (आटा) गूंधना, सानना

kneel - घुटने टेकना, झुकना

knit - बुनना

knock - खटखटाना

knock over - पटकना

know - जानना, पता होना,
  मालूम होना,

known (become ~) -
  पता चलना

L

lack - कमी होना, विहीन होना

laugh - हँसना

lead - आगे-आगे चलना

learn - सीखना, पढ़ना

leave - चल देना

leave, let go - छोड़ना

left (be~) - छूटना

lengthen - लंबा करना

lick - चाटना

lie (tell ~) - झूठ बोलना

lie down - लेटना

lift up - उठाना

light - जलाना

like - पसन्द करना,
  अच्छा लगना (see pg. 122)

limit - सीमित करना

limp - लंगड़ाना

lisp - तोतलाना

listen - (को) सुनना

live (life) - जीना

live (at/in a place) - रहना

load - लादना

loan, lend - उधार देना

locate - स्थापित करना

lock - ताला लगाना

long for - तरसना

look - देखना, नज़र डालना

look after -
(की) देखभाल करना

look around -
(के) आस-पास देखना,
(के) आस-पास खोजना

look for - (की) तलाश करना,
ढूँढ़ना, खोजना

loosen - ढीला करना

lose - खोना

love - (को) प्यार करना,
(को) प्रेम करना

love (be in) - (से) प्यार करना

lower - (के) नीचे उतारना

M

make - बनाना

manifest - प्रदर्शित करना,
प्रकट करना

married (get) -
(की) शादी होना,
(का) विवाह होना

marry - शादी करना,
विवाह करना (कराना)

mature - परिपक्व करना,
पक्का करना

measure - (को) नापना,
नाप लेना

meditate - ध्यान करना

meet - (से) मिलना

melt - पिघलना

memorize - याद करना

mention - (का) ज़िक्र करना

merge - मिलाना, विलीन करना

mess (make ~) - गड़बड़ करना
गड़बड़ कर देना,

mind (take offense) -
बुरा मानना

mischief (make ~) -
शैतानी करना

misinterpret -
(का) गलत अर्थ निकालना

miss - (की) याद आना

mix - (को) मिलाना,
मिश्रण करना

move (go) - चलना

move (object) - हिलाना

mumble - बड़बड़ाना

murder - (की) हत्या करना,
खून करना

mutter - बड़बड़ाना

N

nail - कील लगाना

negate - (को) नकारना,
मना करना

neglect - (पर) ध्यान न देना

negotiate - बात-चीत करना

nibble - कुतरना

noise (make lots of ~) -
शोर मचाना

notice - (पर) ध्यान देना

number - गिनती लगाना,
गिनती करना, अंक लगाना

O

obey - (की) आज्ञा मानना

oblige - बाध्य करना,
मज़बूर करना, कृतज्ञ करना

obtain - मिलना, प्राप्त करना

occur (come to mind) -
सूझना

offer - (का) प्रस्ताव करना

omit - (का) त्याग निकालना

open - खोलना

order (accept ~) -
(का) आदेश मानना

order (call for ~) - मँगवाना

order (give ~) - आदेश देना,
हुक्म देना

organize - प्रबन्ध करना

owe - (का) ऋणी होना,
(का) देनदार होना

own - अपनाना

P

paint - रंग लगाना

pant - साँस फूलना

pardon - (को) क्षमा करना

pass away (die) - गुज़रना

pass time - समय बीतना,
समय व्यतीत करना

pat - थपथपाना

pee - पेशाब करना

peel - छीलना

peep - झाँकना

perceive - समझना

perfect - पूरा करना,
संपन्न करना

perform (music) - बजाना

permeate - व्याप्त करना

permit - आज्ञा देना,
स्वीकार करना

persuade -
(को) विश्वास दिलाना

pervade - व्याप्त करना

photograph - फ़ोटो खींचना,
तस्वीर खींचना

pick - चुनना

pinch - चुटकी काटना, नोचना

place - रखना

plan - योजना करना,
उपाय करना

plant - लगाना

play - खेलना

please - प्रसन्न करना

pluck - तोड़ना

point out - इशारा करना

poke - चुभाना

polish - चमकाना

pollute - (को) गन्दा करना,
(को) मैला करना

possible (be ~) - हो सकना

postpone - टालना,
स्थगित करना, देर करना

pounce - (पर) झपटना

pound - कूटना

pour - डालना

practice - (का) अभ्यास करना

praise - (की) प्रशंसा करना

pray - (की) प्रार्थना करना,
(की) बिनती करना

prefer - ज़्यादा पसंद करना,
अधिक पसंद करना

prepare - (को) तैयार करना
(की) तैयारी करना

present - प्रस्तुत करना,
उपस्थित करना

press - दबाना

pressure (apply ~) -
(पर) दबाव डालना

pretend - बहाना करना,
बहाना बनाना

prevent - रोकना

prick - (को) चुभाना

print - छापना

proceed - आगे चलना,
आगे बढ़ना

proclaim - (की) घोषणा करना

produce - उत्पन्न करना

progress - उन्नति करना

prohibit - निषेध करना,
मना करना

prolong - लम्बा करना

promise - वादा करना,
वचन देना

propose - प्रस्ताव करना

protect - (की) रक्षा करना,
(को) सुरक्षित करना

prove - सिद्ध करना,
प्रमाणित करना

provide - (का) इन्तज़ाम करना

publish - प्रकाशित करना

puff (blow) - फूँक मारना,
फूँकना

pull - खींचना

pulsate - स्फुरण करना,
धड़कना

punish - दण्ड देना, सज़ा देना

purchase - खरीदना

purify - शुद्ध करना,
निर्मल करना

push - ढकेलना, धक्का देना

push away - दूर हटाना

put - रखना

put back - वापस रखना

put in - (में) डालना

put on - पहनना

Q

quarrel - झगड़ना

quench thirst - प्यास बुझाना

quit - त्याग करना, त्यागना,
छोड़ना

R

race - दौड़ना

rain - बरसना, वर्षा होना

raise - उठाना

ramble - बक-बक करना

reach - पहुँचना

read - पढ़ना

ready (be ~) - तैयार करना,
तैयार होना

realize - साक्षात्कार करना

recall - याद करना

receive - प्राप्त करना, मिलना

recognize - पहचानना

recommend - सिफ़ारिश करना

reconsider - फिर सोचना

reduce - कम करना, घटाना

refine - शुद्ध करना

reflect - प्रतिबिम्बित करना

refuse - अस्वीकार करना,
(को) इन्कार करना

reign - राज्य करना

relate - सुनाना

relax - आराम करना, सुस्ताना

release - मुक्त करना,
छुटकारा देना

relish - (का) मज़ा लेना,
(का) मज़ा आना,
(का) स्वाद लेना,
(का) स्वाद आना

remain - रहना, ठहरना,
बना रहना

remember - (को) याद करना

remember (keep in mind) -
याद रखना

remembered (be) - याद होना

remembering (keep) -
याद रहना

remind - याद दिलाना

remove - दूर करना,
दूर हटाना, निवारण करना

renounce - त्याग करना,
छोड़ देना

rent - किराये पर लेना,
  किराये पर देना

repair - ठीक करना,
  मरम्मत करना

repay - पैसा वापस करना

repeat - जपना, दोहराना,
  फिर से करना,
  फिर से कहना

replace - बदलना,
  वापस करना

reply - उत्तर देना

report - ख़बर देना

request - प्रार्थना करना,
  निवेदन करना

rescue - (को) बचाना,
  (की) सहायता करना

resemble - (से) मिलना-जुलना

resent - बुरा मानना

reserve - बचा रखना

reside - रहना, निवास करना

resign - (का) त्यागना

respect - (का) आदर करना,
  (का) सम्मान करना,
  (की) इज़्ज़त करना

respond - उत्तर देना,
  जवाब देना

rest - आराम करना,
  विश्राम करना, सुस्ताना

restrain - रोकना

restrict - सीमित करना

retreat - पीछे हटना

return - लौटना, वापस आना,
  वापस जाना

reveal - व्यक्त करना,
  दिखाई देना

reverse - (को) उल्टा करना

revolve - घुमाना

ride - सवारी करना, चढ़ना

rinse - खंगालना,
  पानी से धोना

rip - फाड़ना

ripen - पकना

rise (stand up) - उठना

rise up - चढ़ना

roam - घूमना, भ्रमण करना

roar - गर्जना

roast - भूनना

roll - लुढ़कना

roll (make ~) - लुढ़काना

rub - रगड़ना

ruin - बरबाद करना, बिगड़ना,
  नाश कर देना

run - दौड़ना

run away - भागना, भाग जाना

rust - जंग लगना

S

sacrifice - बलिदान करना,
  (की) कुर्बानी देना

sag - बैठ जाना

sail - रवाना होना

salute - प्रणाम करना

save - बचाना

saved (be ~) - बचना,
बच जाना

say - कहना

scare - डराना, डरा देना,
चौंकना

scared (be ~) - डरना,
डर जाना

scatter - बिखरना

scheme - योजना बनाना

scold - डाँटना

scold (be scolded) -
(को) डाँट पड़ना

scratch - खुरचना, खुजलाना,
खुजाना

scream - चिल्लाना

search - (को) ढूँढ़ना,
(की) तलाश करना, खोजना

seat - (को) आसन देना

see - देखना

seek - खोजना

seem - लगना, प्रतीत होना,
मालूम होना

seen (be~) - दिखाई देना

seize - पकड़ना

sell - बेचना, बिक्री करना

send - भेजना

senile (go ~) - सठिया जाना

separate - अलग करना

separated (be ~) - अलग होना,
बिछुड़ना

serve - (की) सेवा करना,
(की) नौकरी करना

serve (food) - परोसना, परसना

settle (pay back) - चुकाना

sew - सीना

sewn (be ~) - सिलाना

shade - छाया करना

shake - हिलना, झटकना

share - हिस्सा बाँटना,
हिस्सा करना

shift - स्थान बदलना

shine - चमकना

shiver - काँपना

shock - धक्का लगना

shorten - (को) छोटा करना,
(को) कम करना

shout (shriek) - चीखना

shove - धक्का देना

show - दिखाना

shut - बन्द करना

shut eyes - मूँदना, मूँद लेना

sift - छानना

sing - गाना

sit (see pg. 134) - बैठना

sit (make ~) - (को) बिठाना

slander - (की) निंदा करना

slap - (को) थप्पड़ मारना

sleep - सोना

sleep (go to ~) - सो जाना

sleep (make ~) - सुलाना

sleepy (feel ~) - नींद आना

slide - सरकना

slip - फिसलना

slip away - खिसकना

smash -
(के) टुकड़े-टुकड़े करना

smear - चुपड़ना

smell - सूँघना

smile - मुस्कराना

smoke - (सिगरेट) पीना,
धूम्रपान करना

snap fingers - चुटकी बजाना

snatch - छीनना

sneeze - छींकना

snow - बर्फ़ गिरना, बर्फ़ पड़ना

soak - भिगोना

solve - हल करना,
समाधान करना

sorry (feel ~) -
(का) शोक करना,
(का) खेद करना,
(का) अफ़्सोस करना

sow (seed) - बोना

speak - बोलना

speak loudly - ज़ोर से बोलना,
ऊँचा बोलना

spend - खर्च करना

spend time - बीताना,
गुज़ारना, व्यतीत करना

spill - गिराना

spill (liquid) - छलकना

spin - चक्कर देना

spit - थूकना

split - चीरना, फाड़ना

spoil - बिगाड़ना, ख़राब करना

spoiled (be ~) - बिगड़ना

spread - फैलाना

sprinkle - छिड़कना

squeeze - निचोड़ना

stab - चुभाना

stagger - लड़खड़ाना,
लड़खड़ा जाना

stammer - हकलाना

stand - खड़ा होना

stand (take a ~) - खड़ा करना

stare - (को) घूरना

stare nicely -
(को) एकटक देखना

start - शुरु करना,
आरम्भ करना

start (an action) - लगना
(see Verbs, pg. 118)

startle - चौंकाना, चौंका देना

starve - भूखा रहना

stay - ठहरना, रुकना

steal - चुराना

stick (on) - चिपकाना

sting - डंक मारना

stir - हिलाना, चलाना

stop - रुकना, रोकना

strain - छानना, छनना

strength (apply ~) -
ज़ोर लगाना

strengthen - पक्का करना

stretch - खींचना

stretch (limbs) - अँगड़ाई लेना

strike - मारना, पीटना

struggle - संघर्ष करना

study - पढ़ना

stutter - हकलाना

subtract - घटाना

succeed - सफल करना,
सफल होना

suck - चूसना

suffer - दुःखी रहना,
दुःखी होना

suffer (make ~) -
उदास करना, दुःखी करना

suggest - सुझाव देना

summon - बुलाना

supervise - देखभाल करना

support - (को) सहारा देना

suppose - मान लेना

suppress - दबाना

surrender - समर्पण करना

surround - घेरना

swallow - निगलना

sway - झूलना

swear (an oath) - शपथ लेना

sweat - पसीना आना

sweep - झाड़ू मारना,
झाड़ू लगाना

swell - सूजना

swim - तैरना

swing - झूलना

T

take - लेना

take down - उतारना

take off (clothes) - उतारना

talk - बात करना, बताना

talk idly - बकवास करना

talk non-stop -
बक-बक करना

tangle - उलझाना, उलझना

taste - (का) स्वाद लेना, चखना

teach - पढ़ाना, सिखाना

tear - फाड़ना

tease - छेड़ना

tell - बताना, कहना

tell (a story) - सुनाना

test - परीक्षा लेना

thank - (को) धन्यवाद देना,
(का) धन्यवाद करना

think - सोचना, चिन्तन करना

think of - (की) याद करना

thirst - प्यास लगना

threaten - धमकाना,
धमकी देना

throb - फ़ड़कना, धड़कना

throw - फेंकना

throw (in fire) - झोंकना

throw down - पटक देना

thunder - गरजना

tickle - गुदगुदाना,
गुदगुदी करना

tie - बाँधना

tie together - जोड़ना

tighten - कसना

tire - थकाना, थक जाना

tolerate - सहन करना

touch - (को) छूना, स्पर्श करना

transcend - ऊँचा होना,
ऊपर उठ जाना

transform - परिवर्तन करना,
परिवर्तन होना

translate - भाषान्तर करना,
अनुवाद करना

trap - फँसाना

travel - यात्रा करना

treat - व्यवहार करना

treat (illness) - इलाज करना,
इलाज करवाना

trickle - बूँद-बूँद गिरना

trip - लड़खड़ाना,
लड़खड़ जाना

trouble - परेशान करना

try - (की) कोशीश करना,
(का) प्रयत्न करना

turn - चक्कर देना, फेरना

turn around - मुड़ना, मोड़ना

twinkle - चमकना

twist - मोड़ना, ऐंठना

U

unbutton - बटन खोलना

uncover - ढक्कन हटाना

understand - समझना,
समझ में आना

undress - वस्त्र उतारना

unite - जोड़ना, मिलाना

untie - खोलना

uproot - उखड़ना, उखाड़ना

use - (का) प्रयोग करना,
(का) इस्तेमाल करना

V

verify - प्रमाणित करना,
सच्चा करना, सिद्ध करना

vibrate - काँपना, कम्पन होना

violate - (का) उल्लंघन करना

visible (make ~) - दिखायी देना
visit - भेंट होना, दर्शन करना
visualize - (की) कल्पना करना
vomit - उल्टी करना

W

wag (tail) - हिलाना
wait - (का) इन्तज़ार करना,
     (की) प्रतीक्षा करना
wake up - जागना
walk - पैदल चलना, सैर करना
wander - घूमना, भटकना
want - चाहना
warn - (की) चेतावनी देना
wash - धोना
waste - बरबाद करना,
     नाश करना, क्षय होना
watch - देखना
wave - लहराना
wear - पहनना
weave - बुनना
weep - रोना, रोना-धोना
weigh - तौलना
weight (gain) - वज़न बढ़ना
weight (lose) - वज़न कम करना
     वज़न कम होना
welcome - (का) स्वागत करना
whip - चाबुक लगाना

whisper - फुसफुसाना
     धीरे से बोलना
whistle - सीटी बजाना
win - जीतना, विजयी होना
wink - आँख मारना
wipe - पोंछना
wish - इच्छा करना
wish well - भला करना,
     भला सोचना, भलाई करना
withdraw - हट जाना
wither - मुझना
work - काम करना,
     परिश्रम करना
worry - (की) चिन्ता करना,
     (की) फ़िक्र करना
worship - (की) पूजा करना
wound - ज़ख़्म देना
wrap - ओढ़ना
wreck - नाश करना,
     ख़राब करना
write - लिखना

Y

yawn - जँभाई लेना
yell - चिल्लाना

Conjunctions

Simple Conjunctions

Conjunctions are words used to connect parts of a sentence. A number of conjunctions in Hindi consist of one word and are used in the same way as their English counterparts:

कान्ति और जान्की आज आ रही हैं ।

Kaanti <u>and</u> Jaanki are coming today.

क्या वह अँग्रेज़ी या हिन्दी बोलती है ?

Does she speak English <u>or</u> Hindi?

At the end of a sentence या नहीं means 'or not':

क्या आपके पास पैसा है या नहीं ?

Do you have money <u>or not</u>?

Simple conjunctions are also used to make compound sentences (sentences with two main clauses):

मैं फूल लाती हूँ और वह फल लाती है ।

I bring flowers <u>and</u> she brings fruit.

वह यहाँ आया लेकिन सीता घर पर नहीं थी ।

He came here <u>but</u> Seeta wasn't at home.

हम यह खाना खाना नहीं चाहते क्योंकि वह ख़राब है ।

We don't want to eat this food <u>because</u> it is spoiled.

The conjunction कि is used in the same way as the English 'that':

प्रधान मंत्री ने कहा कि सब ठीक हो जाएगा ।

The Prime Minister said <u>that</u> everything will be all right.

Conjunctions Used in Pairs

Other conjunctions occur in pairs. Two such pairs of conjunctions are used for 'either/or' and 'neither/nor':

हम या तो दिल्ली जाएंगे या वाराणसी ।

> We will go <u>either</u> to Delhi <u>or</u> Varanasi.

मैंने <u>न</u> आराम किया <u>न</u> काम किया ।

> I <u>neither</u> rested <u>nor</u> worked.

This pair चाहे ... या (नहीं) may be used to express an alternative or a choice:

चाहे आप फ़ोन करें या नहीं मैं आ जाऊँगी ।

> I will come <u>whether</u> you phone <u>or</u> not.

हम चाहे मनाली जाएँ, या धर्मशाला, मुझे कोई फ़र्क नहीं पड़ता ।

> <u>Whether</u> we go to Manali <u>or</u> Dharmshaala, it makes no difference to me.

हम कल जाएंगे (चाहे) मौसम अच्छा हो या नहीं ।

> We will go tomorrow <u>whether</u> the weather is good <u>or not</u>.

Two other conjunctions that occur in pairs indicate concession:

हालाँकि हम वहाँ गए थे फिर भी हम लड़की से नहीं मिले ।

> <u>Although</u> we went there, <u>(still)</u> we didn't meet with the girl.

यद्यपि आपने मुझे बताया तथापि मैं भूल गया ।

> <u>Even though</u> you told me, <u>(still)</u> I forgot.

Conditional Sentences ('If' ... 'then')

Two pairs of conjunctions are used to make conditional sentences (अगर...तो and यदि...तो). अगर or यदि introduces the 'if' clause, and तो introduces the 'then' clause.

It is typical to see the subjunctive or future tense in the 'if' clause when the 'then' clause refers to the future:

यदि बसन्त यह काम खत्म न करे तो रवि खत्म करेगा ।

If Basant does not (should not) finish this work, (then) Ravi will (finish it).

अगर हम आज आएंगे तो हम अपनी किताबें साथ लाएंगे ।

If we (will) come today, (then) we will bring our books.

The verb in the 'if' clause may also be a perfect participle (देखा, किया, etc.) or in the present imperfect tense (देखता हूँ, करता हूँ, etc.):

यदि उसने अब तक नहीं किया है तो वह कभी नहीं करेगा ।

If he hasn't done it by now, (then) he will never do it.

यदि आप कुछ फल चाहते हैं तो मैं आपको सेब और केले दूँगा ।

If you want some fruit, (then) I will give you apples and bananas.

It is also possible to have an imperative or subjunctive verb form in the 'then' clause:

अगर खाना तैयार हो तो मुझे कुछ लाइए ।

If the food is ready, (then) bring me some.

यदि आप मकान बनाएं तो मैं उसको शायद खरीदूँ ।

If you build a house, (then) I might buy it.

Sentences of the general form 'if it were so, then... ,' which refer to unrealized or unlikely conditions, are expressed by conditional sentences in which the verbs in both clauses are imperfect participles (देखता, करता, etc.):

यदि वह दयालु होता तो वह दान देता ।

If he were kind, he would give to charity.[1]

यदि हम उसका पता जानते तो उसको पत्र लिखते ।

If we knew his address, we would write him a letter.

अगर माता-जी यहाँ नहीं होती तो बच्चे कभी अपना
काम नहीं करते ।

If mother were not here, the children would never
do their work.

If reference is to the past, as in 'had it been so, then...,' the 'if' clause takes the perfect participle followed by the imperfect participle of होना (होता, होती, होते etc.); the verb in the 'then' clause is an imperfect participle:

यदि आप ठीक समय पर आए होते तो मैं आपकी पसंद का
खाना बनाती ।

If you had arrived on time, I would have prepared the
food of your choice.

यदि मैंने राम से नहीं पूछा होता तो मैं आपसे पूछता ।

If I hadn't asked Raam, I would have asked you.

---

[1] Sometimes यदि 'if' is dropped in this (and the following) kind of conditional sentence.

Relative-Correlative Structures

Sentences formed using relative-correlative structures consist of a main clause and a relative clause. A relative clause contains a relative pronoun, adverb, or adjective which functions as a placeholder for a pronoun, adverb, or adjective (called the correlative) in the main clause. In Hindi the order of the clauses is usually reversed.

Consider the sentence:

<u>I will go</u>	<u>where the sun shines</u>
main clause	relative clause

in which the relative clause contains the relative adverb 'where.' In Hindi the main clause contains a correlative adverb 'there' which is paired up with the relative adverb 'where':

<u>Where</u> the sunshine is,	<u>there</u> I will go.
जहाँ धूप होती है	वहाँ मैं जाऊँगा ।

There are many relative-correlative pairs like 'where...there...' in Hindi. Relative-correlative pairs for time, place, and manner are given in the following examples:

जब मैं वापस आऊँगा, तब माता जी को बुलाइए ।

Call Mom when I get back.

(<u>When</u> I (will) come back, <u>then</u> call Mom.)

जब भी मेरी बहन आती है, तभी मैं केक बनाती हूँ ।

I make cake whenever my sister comes.

(<u>Whenever</u> my sister comes, <u>then</u> I make cake.)

जब तक वह गा रही थी, तब तक बच्चे यहाँ रहे ।

The children stayed here as long as she was singing.

(<u>As long</u> as she was singing, <u>until then</u> the children stayed here.)

जैसा आप चाहें, वैसा कीजिए ।

Do as you like. (Just as you may want, in that way do.)

जितना पैसा उसके पास है, उतना मेरे पास है ।

I have as much money as he has.

(As much money as he has, that much I have.)

जहाँ उसकी माता जी जाती हैं, वहाँ बेटी भी जाना चाहती है ।

The daughter also wants to go where her mother goes.

(Where her mother goes, there the daughter also wants to go.)

The Relative Pronoun जो

The relative pronoun in Hindi is जो 'the one(s) who/which/ that.' Its correlative counterpart is usually वह or वे (or some form of these pronouns). जो is both singular and plural:

जो पढ़ता है, वह सीखता है ।

He who studies, (he) learns.

जो पढ़ते हैं, वे सीखते हैं ।

Those who study, (they) learn.

जो हिन्दी बोलना चाहता है, उसको बहुत पढ़ना पड़ेगा ।

He who wants to speak Hindi, (he) will have to study a lot.

जो कपड़ा मेज़ पर है, वह मुझे चाहिए ।

I want the cloth which is on the table.

(The cloth which is on the table, that (one) I want.)

The oblique case of जो is जिस in the singular and जिन in the plural:

जिसको खाना चाहिए, उसको बुलाइए ।

Call the one who wants food.

(The one who wants food, call him.)

जिस लड़के से आप बोल रहे थे, वह समझदार है ।

The boy you were speaking with is intelligent.

(The boy with whom you were speaking, he is intelligent.)

जिन लोगों को मैंने कल देखा, वे आज नहीं आ सकते ।

The people I saw yesterday can't come today.

(The people whom I saw yesterday, they can't come today.)

Simple Conjunctions

and - और, तथा

as well as - एवम्

because - क्योंकि, चूंकि

but - लेकिन, परन्तु, मगर, किन्तु, पर

but also - बल्कि

but even so - तो भी

if not, then, unless - नहीं तो

or - या, अथवा

otherwise - नहीं तो, वरना

rather - बल्कि, अथवा

so - तो

so that - ताकि

still - फिर भी

still then - तो भी

that - कि

that is, i.e. - यानी

then, so - तो

therefore - इसलिए

would that...(how I wish that...) - काश (~कि)

yet - फिर भी

Conjunctions Used in Pairs

Although... यद्यपि, हालाँकि

If... यदि, अगर

Whether, no matter... चाहे

even still... तथापि, फिर भी, तो भी

then, so... तो

or not... या नहीं

Relative

As long as... जब तक

As many... As much...
जितना

As soon as... जैसे ही, ज्योंहि

Just as, just like, as... जैसा

Since... जब से

The one who/which... जो

oblique case, sing. of जो - जिस

oblique case, pl. of जो - जिन

Whatever... जो कुछ

When... जब

Whenever... जब ही, जब

Where... जहाँ

Wherever... जहाँ भी

Whichever... जो कोई

While... जबकि

Whoever... जो कोई

Correlative

until then... तब तक

that many... that much...
उतना

that soon... वैसे ही, त्योंहि

in that way, so... वैसा

since then... तब से

he, she, it, that... वह,
they... वे

oblique case of वह - उस

oblique case of वे - उन

it, that... वह

then... तब

then... तब भी, तब

there... वहाँ

there... वहाँ भी

he, she, it, that one... वह

then... तब

he, she, it, that one... वह

Note: In this list, a capital letter indicates that the conjunction in question usually appears at the beginning of the sentence.

Miscellaneous

Interjections/Salutations

The same word is used to say both 'hello' and 'goodbye' in Hindi. The most frequently used forms are नमस्ते and नमस्कार.

धन्यवाद (literally, 'good fortune') is used to say, 'Thank you!'

Other interjections are:

हाँ	Yes	शाबाश !	Well done! Splendid!
बस !	Stop! Enough!	मुबारक !	Blessings!

The Honorific Particle जी

जी is a word that one hears and uses a lot in Hindi. If it is added to a name it denotes respect, but also familiarity. You may use it freely in conversation:

नमस्ते सीता-जी ।   Hello Seetaa-jee.

It is also usually added to the words 'yes' and 'no'. Its absence may even seem odd to the listener:

हाँ जी or जी हाँ   Yes
नहीं जी or जी नहीं   No

जी used alone also means 'yes.'

The Emphatic Particle ही

The particle ही adds emphasis to the word or words that precede it. Its sense varies somewhat depending on its context. It is best understood by examples:

वह एक ही बार आया ।	He came <u>only</u> one time.
यह किताब बहुत ही पुरानी है ।	This book is <u>really</u>/<u>very</u> old.
दुकान पास ही है ।	The store is <u>just</u> nearby.
मैं ही जा रहा हूँ ।	<u>Only</u> I am going.

ही is used with all forms of pronouns in the direct and oblique cases. Some pronouns, but not all, change their forms when ही is added(e.g., मुझ + ही = मुझी 'only me,' 'just me,' etc.):

Direct Case	Oblique Case
मैं + ही = मैं ही	मुझ + ही = मुझी
तू + ही = तू ही	तुझ + ही = तुझी
वह + ही = वही	उस + ही = उसी
यह + ही = यही	इस + ही = इसी
हम + ही = हमीं	हम + ही = हमीं
तुम + ही = तुम्हीं	तुम + ही = तुम्हीं
आप + ही = आप ही	आप + ही = आप ही
वे + ही = वे ही	उन + ही = उन्हीं
ये + ही = ये ही	इन + ही = इन्हीं

मुझे वही किताब चाहिए ।	I need <u>that very</u> book.
उसी लड़के को बुलाइए ।	Invite <u>only that</u> boy.

ही combines with some adverbs to stress importance or immediacy:

अब (now) + ही = अभी	right now
यहाँ (here) + ही = यहीं	right here
वहाँ (there) + ही = वहीं	right there
सब (all) + ही = सभी	all (emphatic)

When ही is meant to convey the meaning 'only' it is not combined with the adverb:

यहाँ ही only here

Other Uses of तो

In addition to the uses noted earlier (see Conjunctions pg. 165), तो is also used to provide emphasis or contrast, as illustrated by the following examples:

Meaning 'so' or 'then' (indicating contrast or continuity with a preceding idea):

ठीक है, तो मत जाइए !	Okay, then don't go!
अच्छा, तो हम करेंगे ।	All right, we'll do it.
तो, क्या हुआ ?	So, what happened?

As an emphatic:

बात तो यह है कि...	The fact *is* that…
किताब तो मिली, पर कलम नहीं ।	The *book* was found, but not the pen.
आप अच्छे तो हैं ?	Are you (actually) well?

As a slight protest:

मैं तो गया था !	(But) I did go!
राज कमल को तो बुलाओ !	(Just) call Raj Kamal!

Following नहीं meaning 'otherwise':

अपना खाना अभी खाओ नहीं तो मैं चला जाऊँगा ।	Eat your food right now, otherwise I will go.

The Suffix वाला

The suffix वाला 'the one who, the one which' is especially common in informal speech. वाला is added to nouns, adverbs, and the oblique infinitive of verbs to form nouns and adjectives such as the following:

With nouns:

दूध-वाला	milkman	दूध-वाली	milkwoman
चाय-वाला	tea maker	टैक्सी-वाला	taxi driver
गाँव-वाला	villager (male)	गाँव-वाली	villager (female)
टोपी वाला (आदमी)		the man with the hat	
		(use of आदमी is optional)	

With adverbs:

ऊपर वाला	the one upstairs
नीचे वाला	the one downstairs
पास वाला	the one nearby

With oblique infinitives:

देखने वाला	spectator
बोलने वाला	speaker
जाने वाला	the one about to go
आने वाला	upcoming, the one about to come
दिल्ली का रहने वाला	resident of Delhi
भारत का रहने वाला	citizen of India

The Use of भर

Following a noun, भर means 'the total amount of' or 'the whole of':

दिन भर	the whole day
रात भर	the whole night
पेट भर	full (to capacity) stomach
देश भर	the entire country
घर भर	the whole house

Uses of ऐसा

The adjective and adverb ऐसा 'of this kind, in this way, etc.' is used in a number of frequently heard expressions. Some typical examples are given below. Notice that in these expressions the pronoun वह 'it' is understood but not stated:

ऐसा है ।	It is so.
ऐसा नहीं है।	It is not so.
ऐसा ही है ।	It is just like this.
ऐसा ही रहने दो !	Let it be!
ऐसा ही हुआ ।	It happened just like that.
ऐसा करना ।	Do it like this.
ऐसा करना मना है ।	It is forbidden to do this.
ऐसा नहीं हो सकता ।	It can't be so.

Repeated Words

The repetition of words is quite common in Hindi. Pronouns, adjectives, and adverbs may be repeated, usually to convey a sense of distribution or distinction.

Pronouns

आज कौन कौन आया ?	Who (what different people) came today?
आप क्या क्या काम करते हैं ?	What (different kinds of) work do you do?
उसने क्या क्या बनाया ?	What (different things) did he prepare?
कोई कोई आता है, कोई कोई नहीं आता ।	Some (kinds of people) come and some don't.

Adjectives and Adverbs

अपना अपना काम करो ।	(Each of you) do your own work.
सारी चीज़ें अलग अलग कीजिए ।	Separate all the (different) things.
ये कपड़े कितने कितने पैसे के हैं ?	How much do (each of) these clothes cost?
वे कहाँ कहाँ जाएंगे?	Where (to which different places) will they go?

Repetition of adjectives and adverbs sometimes adds emphasis:

वह बड़ा बड़ा मकान है !	That is a (really) big house!
वह धीरे धीरे चलता है ।	He moves (really) slowly.

Repetition of numerals is also common, as in दो दो 'two at a time' or 'two each':

सब लड़कियाँ दो दो गीत गाएँगी ।	All the girls will sing two songs (each).
चिड़िया ने एक एक तिनका लेकर घोंसला बनाया ।	The bird took one blade of grass at a time and built a nest.

Reported Speech

In Hindi, reporting of thoughts, statements, or questions can be done by repeating the actual words thought or spoken. The conjunction कि normally introduces the quoted speech:

उसने कहा कि मैं नहीं आऊँगा ।	He said he would not come. (He said, "I will not come.")
उन्होंने मुझसे पूछा कि आपका नाम क्या है ?	They asked me what my name is. (They asked from me (that), "What is your name?")
मेरा विचार था कि मैं आपको मिलूँ ।	I thought that I should meet you.
क्या आप सोचते हैं कि हीरा असली है ?	Do you think that the diamond is real?

Another way of saying this is to follow the pattern:

उसने कहा कि वह नहीं आएगा ।	He said that he would not come.
कुमार समझता है कि मैं आज नहीं जा सकता ।	Kumaar understands that I can't go today.

Sometimes such sentences may be ambiguous, since there is no way to determine whether the reported speech is being directly quoted or not. In such cases the context of the sentence or speech should resolve the ambiguity.

Reporting of commands also follows this pattern; however, the verb in the command is usually in the subjunctive rather than the imperative form:

अपने भाई से कहो कि
वह घर वापस आए ।

Tell your brother to come home. (Tell your brother that he should come home.)

माता-जी ने बच्चे से कहा कि
वह अभी जाए ।

Mother told the child to go right now.

Especially common with reported commands involving जाना 'to go' is the following construction in which the oblique case infinitive of जाना is used with को:

अपनी बहन से दुकान जाने
को कहो ।

Tell your sister to go to the store.

पिता-जी ने मुझे सो जाने
को कहा ।

Dad told me to go to sleep.

It also applies to other verbs:

उसे खाने को कहो ।

Tell him to eat.

Days of the Week

Monday	सोमवार
Tuesday	मंगलवार
Wednesday	बुधवार
Thursday	गुरुवार, बृहस्पतिवार
Friday	शुक्रवार
Saturday	शनिवार
Sunday	रविवार, इतवार

References to days of the week usually take the postposition को (e.g., हम सोमवार को मिलेंगे । We'll meet on Monday).

सारा दिन/दिन भर	all day
प्रतिदिन/रोज़-रोज़	every day, daily
कल	yesterday, tomorrow
परसों	the day before yesterday, the day after tomorrow
आज-कल	these days
एक साल पहले	a year ago
दो हफ़्ते पहले	two weeks ago

Time of Day

The verb बजना (literally, 'to chime') is used to express time:

1:00	एक बजा	7:00	सात बजे
2:00	दो बजे	8:00	आठ बजे
3:00	तीन बजे	9:00	नौ बजे
4:00	चार बजे	10:00	दस बजे
5:00	पाँच बजे	11:00	ग्यारह बजे
6:00	छः बजे	12:00	बारह बजे

midnight - आधी रात

quarter past the hour - सवा   e.g., 3:15 - सवा तीन बजे

half past the hour - साढ़े   e.g., 3:30 - साढ़े तीन बजे

quarter to the hour - पौने   e.g., 3:45 - पौने चार बजे

Note the following exceptions:

1:15   सवा बजा

1:30   डेढ़ बजा

2:30   ढाई बजे

Minutes before and after the hour are expressed using बजने में (before the hour) and बजकर (after the hour):

तीन बजने में दस मिनट   ten minutes to three

तीन बजकर बीस मिनट   twenty minutes past three

Divisions of the Day

सुबह जल्दी, सुबह-सुबह	early morning
सुबह को	morning (daybreak to middday)
दोपहर को	midday
दिन को	day (midday to 4 p.m.)
शाम को	evening (from 4 p.m. to 8 p.m.)
रात को	night (8 p.m. to daybreak)

These divisions can play the same role as a.m. and p.m. in English:

छ: बजे सुबह को	6:00 a.m.
सुबह के दस बजे	10:00 a.m.
दिन के तीन बजे	3:00 p.m.
दिन के पौने चार बजे	3:45 p.m.
पाँच बजे शाम को	5:00 p.m.
दो बजे रात को	2:00 a.m.

Some Expressions of Time

कितने बजे हैं?	What is the time?
साढ़े तीन बजे हैं।	It is three thirty.
काफ़ी समय है।	There is enough (plenty of) time.
सुबह के दस बजने वाले हैं।	It is nearly 10:00 a.m.
ठीक दस बजे रात को।	exactly 10:00 p.m. (on the dot)
हमें देर हो गई।	We were late. (To us lateness became.)

0	शून्य	23	तेईस	51	इक्यावन	79	उनासी
¼	सवा	24	चौबीस	52	बावन	80	अस्सी
½	आधा	25	पच्चीस	53	त्रेपन	81	इक्यासी
¾	पौना	26	छब्बीस	54	चौवन	82	बयासी
1	एक	27	सत्ताईस	55	पचपन	83	तिरासी
1½	डेढ़	28	अट्ठाईस	56	छप्पन	84	चौरासी
2	दो	29	उनतीस	57	सत्तावन	85	पचासी
2½	ढाई	30	तीस	58	अट्ठावन	86	छियासी
3	तीन	31	इक्त्तीस	59	उनसठ	87	सत्तासी
4	चार	32	बत्तीस	60	साठ	88	अट्ठासी
5	पाँच	33	तैंतीस	61	इक्सठ	89	नवासी
6	छ:	34	चौंतीस	62	बासठ	90	नब्बे
7	सात	35	पैंतीस	63	त्रेसठ	91	इक्यानवे
8	आठ	36	छत्तीस	64	चौंसठ	92	बानवे
9	नौ	37	सैंतीस	65	पैंसठ	93	तिरानवे
10	दस	38	अड़तीस	66	छियासठ	94	चौरानवे
11	ग्यारह	39	उन्तालीस	67	सरसठ	95	पच्यानवे
12	बारह	40	चालीस	68	अड़सठ	96	छियानवे
13	तेरह	41	इकतालीस	69	उनहत्तर	97	सत्तानवे
14	चौदह	42	बयालीस	70	सत्तर	98	अट्ठानवे
15	पन्द्रह	43	तैंतालीस	71	इकहत्तर	99	निन्यानवे
16	सोलह	44	चवालीस	72	बहत्तर	100	एक सौ
17	सत्तरह	45	पैंतालीस	73	तिहत्तर	1000	
18	अठारह	46	छियालीस	74	चौहत्तर		एक हज़ार
19	उन्नीस	47	सैंतालीस	75	पचहत्तर	100,000	
20	बीस	48	अड़तालीस	76	छियत्तर		एक लाख
21	इक्कीस	49	उन्चास	77	सतहत्तर	10 million	
22	बाईस	50	पचास	78	अठत्तर		एक करोड़

Hindi Numerals

0 -	०
1 -	१
2 -	२
3 -	३
4 -	४
5 -	५
6 -	६
7 -	७
8 -	८
9 -	९

Ordinal Numbers

पहला	first
दूसरा	second
तीसरा	third
चौथा	fourth
पाँचवाँ	fifth
छठा	sixth
सातवाँ	seventh
आठवाँ	eighth
नवाँ	ninth
दसवाँ	tenth

The other ordinal numbers are formed by adding वाँ to the end of the number.

Aggregates

दोनों	both, the two
तीनों	(all) three

Other aggregates are formed by adding ओं to the end of the number.

दसों	(all) ten
दर्जनों	dozens of
सैंकड़ों	hundreds of
हज़ारों	thousands of
लाखों	hundreds of thousands of
करोड़ों	tens of millions

Useful Expressions

Good morning!	शुभ प्रभात ।
Good night!	शुभ रात्रि ।
Hello!	नमस्ते, नमस्कार
Goodbye!	नमस्ते, नमस्कार
We will meet again.	फिर मिलेंगे ।
Take care of your health.	अपनी तबियत का ध्यान रखिए ।
Thank you.	धन्यवाद ।
Are you free?	क्या आपको फुर्सत है ?
Be quiet.	शान्त रहिए । चुप रहिए ।
Be happy.	खुश रहिए ।
Can you tell me?	क्या आप मुझे बता सकते हैं ?
Congratulations!	बधाई! बधाई हो !
Convey my regards.	मेरा प्रणाम कहें ।
Could you speak clearly?	क्या आप साफ-साफ बोल सकते हैं ?
Do one thing.	एक काम करो ।
Do me a favor.	मेरा एक काम कीजिए ।
Don't worry.	चिन्ता मत करो ।
Excuse me.	माफ करो । माफ कीजिए । क्षमा करें ।
Go away!	जाइए ! जाओ ! भाग जाओ !
Happy Birthday.	जन्म दिन के लिए शुभ कामनाएँ । जन्म दिन मुबारक हो ।
Have a nice journey.	आपकी यात्रा सुखमय हो । आपकी यात्रा शुभ हो ।
Have a nice time.	अच्छा समय व्यतीत हो ।

How are you?	आपका क्या हाल है ?
	आप कैसे हैं ?
I am fine.	मैं ठीक हूँ ।
So so.	ठीक ही है ।
Everything is good.	सब कुछ ठीक है ।
How long will it take?	कितना समय लगेगा?
How old are you?	आपकी उम्र क्या है?
	आपकी आयु कितनी है ?
How was your trip?	आपकी यात्रा कैसी थी?
I agree with you.	मैं आपसे सहमत हूँ ।
I am late.	मुझे देर हो गई ।
I am pleased.	मुझे बहुत खुशी हुई ।
I am pleased to meet you.	मुझे आपसे मिलकर
	बहुत खुशी हुई ।
I am sorry.	मुझे अफ़सोस है ।
I am surprised.	मुझे आश्चर्य है ।
I believe.	मुझे विश्वास है ।
I came to know.	मुझे पता चला ।
I don't mind.	मैं बुरा नहीं मानता / मानती ।
I get nervous.	मुझे घबराहट होती है ।
I got confused.	मैं दुविधा में पड़ गया / गई ।
I have no interest in it.	मुझे इसमें कोई दिलचस्पी
	नहीं है ।
I hope/wish.	मुझे आशा है ।
I know.	मुझे पता है । मुझे मालूम है ।
I like.	मुझे पसन्द है ।
I remember.	मुझे याद है ।

I think so.	मेरा ऐसा ख्याल है ।
I don't think so.	मेरा ऐसा ख्याल नहीं है ।
	मेरा ऐसा विचार नहीं है ।
I also think so.	मेरा भी यह ख्याल है ।
	मेरा भी यह विचार है ।
I want to ask you a favor.	मैं आपको एक कष्ट देना चाहता हूँ ।
	मुझे आपसे एक काम है ।
I wish you joy.	आप खुश रहें ।
I want to ask that...	मैं पूछना चाहता / चाहती हूँ कि ... ।
I'm in a hurry.	मैं जल्दी में हूँ ।
I'm not sure.	मुझे पक्का पता नहीं है ।
If it is not too much trouble...	यदि आपको कष्ट न हो तो... ।
It all depends on God.	भगवान की इच्छा है ।
It does not matter.	कोई बात नहीं ।
It is true.	यह सच है ।
It is unbelievable.	विश्वास नहीं होता ।
It is impossible.	यह असम्भव है ।
It should be good.	अच्छा होना चाहिए ।
It was unexpected.	इसकी आशा नहीं थी ।
Leave me alone.	मुझे अकेला छोड़ दो ।
Make sure to do it.	यह ज़रूर करना है ।
My advice is...	मेरी सलाह यह है... ।
My sympathy is with them.	मेरी उनसे सहानुभूति है ।
Please have this cooked more.	अच्छी तरह पकाकर लाइए ।
Say it again (slowly).	(धीरे से) फिर कहिए ।
	फिर से कहिए ।

There is not even elbow room.	हाथ हिलाने की ही जगह नहीं है ।
There is plenty of time.	काफ़ी समय है ।
What a coincidence!	क्या इत्तफ़ाक़ है !
What a joy.	कैसी खुशी है। । क्या आनन्द है ।
What a nice scene.	कैसा सुन्दर दृश्य है ।
What could I do for you?	मैं आपके लिए क्या कर सकता / सकती हूँ?
What do you mean?	आपका क्या मतलब है? क्या मतलब है?
What happened?	क्या हुआ?
What is your name?	आपका नाम क्या है?
My name is ...	मेरा नाम ... है ।
What is the matter?	क्या बात है?
What's happening?	क्या हो रहा है?
You are right	आप ठीक कहते हैं ।

Food Items

Various

butter	(m)	मक्खन
chick pea	(m)	चना
cornflour	(m)	मक्की की आटा
curd	(m)	दही
lentil	(f)	दाल
green lentil	(m)	मूँग
kidney bean	(m)	राजमाश
maize corn	(m)	मक्की
oil	(m)	तेल
porridge	(m)	दलिया
rice	(m)	चावल
semolina	(f)	सूजी
sugar	(f)	चीनी
tea	(f)	चाय
vinegar	(m)	सिरका
white flour	(m)	मैदा
whole wheat flour		
	(m)	आटा

Spices (m) मसाला

ajwain	(f)	अजवायन
black pepper	(f)	काली मिर्च
cardamon	(f)	इलायची
cinnamon	(f)	दाल चीनी
cloves	(f)	लौंग
coriander	(f)	धनिया
cumin	(m)	जीरा
fenugreek	(m)	मेथी
garam masala	(m)	गरम मसाला
ginger	(m)	अदरक
green mango powder		
	(m)	आम चूर
mint	(m)	पुदीना
mustard seeds		
	(f)	सरसों, राई
salt	(m)	नमक
sesame	(m)	तिल
tamarind	(f)	इमली
turmeric	(f)	हल्दी

Fruits (m) फल

almond	(m)	बादाम
apple	(m)	सेब
apricot	(f)	खुर्मानी
banana	(m)	केला
cashew	(m)	काजु
grape	(m)	अंगूर
guava	(m)	अमरूद
honey	(m)	शहद
lemon	(m)	नीबू / निम्बू
mango	(m)	आम
orange	(m)	संतरा
papaya	(m)	पपीता
peach	(m)	आड़ू
peanut	(f)	मूँगफ़ली
pear	(f)	नाशपाती
pineappple	(f)	अनन्नास
pistachio	(m)	पिस्ता
plum	(m)	आलू-बुखारा
pomegranate	(f)	अनार
raisin	(f)	किशमिश
walnuts	(m)	अखरोट
water-melon	(m)	तरबूज़

Vegetables (f.pl.) सब्ज़ियाँ

beet root	(m)	चुकन्दर
cabbage	(f)	बन्द गोभी
carrot	(f)	गाजर
cauliflower	(f)	फूल गोभी
chilli	(f)	मिर्च
cucumber	(m)	खीरा
eggplant	(m)	बैंगन
green pepper	(f)	शिमला मिर्च
greens	(m)	साग
onion	(f)	प्याज़
peas	(m)	मटर
potato	(m)	आलू
pumpkin	(m.)	कद्दू
radish	(f)	मूली
spinach	(m)	पालक
sweet potato	(m)	शकरकन्दी
tomatoes	(m)	टमाटर
turnip	(m)	शलग़म

Family Relations[1]

mother		माता		
father		पिता		
sister		बहन		
elder sister		दीदी		
brother		भाई, भैया		
elder brother		बड़े भैया		
father-in-law		ससुर		
mother-in-law		सास		
daughter-in-law		बहू		
son-in-law		दामाद		

sister-in-law

    (husband's sister)   ननद

    (wife's sister)   साली

brother-in-law

    (husband's elder brother)   जेठ

    (husband's younger brother)   देवर

    (wife's brother)   साला

uncle	(paternal)	चाचा	(maternal)	मामा
aunt	(paternal)	चाची	(maternal)	मामी
grandfather	(paternal)	दादा	(maternal)	नाना
grandmother	(paternal)	दादी	(maternal)	नानी
grandson	(son's son)	पोता	(daughter's son)	नाती

granddaughter

    (son's daughter)   पोती

    (daughter's daughter)   नातिन

---

[1] Recall that English sentences such as, 'Chaytna has four brothers,' are expressed in Hindi using postpositions. (चेतना के चार भाई हैं ।) See Postpositions pg. 89.

A

aanaa आना (to come) with को, 120, 123, 124

aashaa आशा (hope), 120

achchhaa laganaa अच्छा लगना (like), 122

Adjectives

    about, 31-34

    Dictionary Listings, 35-47

    Ending in आ, 31

    Like, similar to सा, 34

    Making Comparisons, 33

    Not ending in आ, 32

    Plural, 31, 49

    Possessive अपना (one's own), 26

    with Oblique Case Nouns, 32

Adverbs

    about, 93-94

    Devices to form adverbs (से, रूप से, पूर्वक), 94

    Dictionary Listings, 95-100

    how कैसे, 93

    Interrogative, 93

    what क्या, 93

    when कब, 93

    where कहाँ, 93

    why क्यों, 93

agar अगर (if), 165

Aggregates, Numbers, 185

aisaa ऐसा (in this way, of this kind), 177

allow (to) देना, 118

and और, 33, 163, 170

apanaa अपना (one's own), 26, 29

apanay aap, swayam, khud, etc. अपने आप,

    स्वयं, खुद (one's own self), 25

Arrangement of Sounds, *Dev Naagari*, 10

Aspirated letters, 19, 21

aur और (and), 33, 163, 170

D

P

pardanaa, पड़ना
    Compound Verbs, 133
    fall (to), 135
    lie (to), 135
    must, 122
    Transitive and Intransitive Uses of, 116

Participles
    हुआ, हुई, हुए, 138-139
    Adjectival Use, 138
    Adverbial Uses, 139
    with Passive Voice, 126

pasand पसन्द (like), 122

Passive Voice, 126

peenaa पीना (to drink)
    Irregular Forms, 104, 115

Perfect Tenses, 110-116
    Intransitive Verbs, 111-112
    Irregular Perfect Participles, 115
    Irregular Perfect Participles of जाना (to go), 112
    Transitive Verbs, 113-116

perhaps शायद, संभव, 110

period, Hindi, 14

Physical Conditions, 123
    ठंड, जुकाम cold, चक्कर dizziness, बुखार fever,
    भूख hunger, चोट hurt, प्यास thirst

Plural — Direct Case Nouns, 49

poochhanaa पूछना (to ask), with से, 134

Possessive
    Adjective अपना (one's own), 26, 29
    Pronouns (my, yours, etc.), 24, 26, 27

Postpositions
    about, 85-90
    Compound Postpositions (in front of, etc.), 86
    Dictionary Listings, 91-92

Let's Learn Hindi

Dev Naagari Handwritten Alphabet

Vowels

अ आ इ ई
उ ऊ ऋ ए ऐ
ओ औ अं अः

Consonants

क ख ग घ ङ
च छ ज झ ञ
ट ठ ड ढ ण
त थ द ध न
प फ ब भ म
य र ल व
श ष स
ह
क्ष त्र ज्ञ

Reading Exercises for Audio CD

Two, three, and four letter words:
मन, जब, सच, यश, ऐनक, बहन, झगड़, मरण, झट-पट, लगभग अनपढ़

(mind, when, truth, fame, glasses, sister, fight, death, immediately, approximately, illiterate)

Words with आ *maatraa*:
बाल, हरा, कान, ज्ञान, माता, आया, दवाई, चाचा, पढ़ना, खाओ!

(hair, green, ear, knowledge, mother, came, medicine, uncle, read, Eat!)

Words with इ *maatraa*:
बिना, मित्र, दिया, हिरन, किताब, विकास, विषय, हिसाब, बढ़िया, शिकायत

(without, friend, gave, deer, book, development, subject, account, nice, complaint)

Words with ई *maatraa*:
पक्षी, भीड़, घड़ी, थाली, जीवन, मीठी, लड़की, पिता-जी, तितली, इलायची

(bird, crowd, watch, plate, life, sweet, girl, father, butterfly, cardamom)

Words with उ *maatraa*:
मुझ, छुआ, धनुष, घुटना, गुलाबी, मधुर, बुखार, दुनिया, जादुई, रुपया

(me, touched, rainbow, knee, pink, sweet, fever, world, magical, money)

Words with ऊ *maatraa*:
रूप, झूला, सूखा, छूना, ऊपर, झाड़ू, तराज़ू, दूसरा, थूकना, खूबसूरत

(form, swing, dry, touch, above, broom, scale, second, spit, beautiful)

Words with ऋ *maatraa*:
हृदय, वृक्ष, दृढ़, गृह, कृपया, कृति, ऋषि, पृथक, दृढ़ता, घृणा

(heart, tree, firm, home, please, creation, sage, separate, firmness, aversion)

Words with ए *maatraa*:
शेर, पीछे, मुझे, अनेक, लेना, सहेली, देखना, विदेशी, देख-भाल, ढकेलना

(lion, behind, to me, many, take, girlfriend, see, foreigner, care, push)

Words with ऐ *maatraa*:
कैसा, थैला, मैदान, अवैध, फैलना, तैयार, हैरान, बैठना, दैनिक, कैदखाना

(how, bag, field, illegal, spread, ready, amazed, sit, daily, jail)

Words with ओ *maatraa*:
सुनो, बैठो, कोई, तोड़ना, छोटा, मनोहर, थोड़ी, दोहरा, रसोई, छोड़ना

(Listen! Sit! any, break, small, charming, small, double, kitchen, leave)

Words with औ *maatraa*:
शौक, यौवन, मौसम, नौकर, मौजूद, चौदह, मौसी, पकौड़ा, लौटना, खिलौना

(pleasure, youth, weather, servant, available, fourteen, aunt, pakora, return, toy)

Words with अं, अः *maatraas*:
हैं, ढंग, मुँह, वहाँ, नहीं, अहं, सिंधु, हँसना, किताबें, हिंदी, छः, दुःख

(are, manner, mouth, there, not, self, ocean, laugh, books, Hindi, six, pain)

What the world says about
Let's Learn Hindi

From a professional medical practitioner:

Learning a foreign language such as Hindi can be both difficult and stressful for most people. Having such a clear, well-laid out, easily accessible, user friendly learning resource has made the subject interesting and enjoyable to learn. As a recent student of Hindi I can personally attest to its practical and useful nature by the number of times I have used **Let's Learn Hindi**!

Gary Miller MD FRCPC
AMIH Clinic
Kullu, India

From a language student:

There are many Hindi language courses and 'teach yourself' books available and some are quite good. Whether you use other course material or not, **Let's Learn Hindi** is a godsend to both the beginning student and those who are looking for an easy means of refreshing their knowledge of Hindi. It is the ultimate in user friendliness, so much so that it makes you want to learn.

John Davidson
Communications Consultant
London, England

From a 30-year foreign resident in the Indian Himalayas:

Hindi is a magnificent language. To really learn Hindi is to see with a different vision, and those of us from the west who can do so are rare. Rarer still are teachers who can show you how to use the language. Ms. Feinstein has not only mastered that vision, she has spent many years refining her communication of it as a teacher and personal tutor. Her work is a magnificent accomplishment, and a boon to anyone wishing to learn to speak this language.

Don de Belle
Computer Programmer
Montreal, Canada

What the world says about
Let's Learn Hindi

From a university language professor:

I have been using **Let's Learn Hindi** in several of my courses at Harvard University with great success. Because it is such a 'user-friendly' quick reference grammar book and dictionary, students have found it an invaluable supplement to the other language and literature texts I use in my courses. Several students have found the grammar explanations to be accessible as they are written in a simple language and avoid the use of excessive linguistic terms and jargons.

Since I teach both the Urdu and Hindi scripts in my courses, students have also found **Let's Learn Hindi** most useful as a guide to Hindi orthography. I would enthusiastically recommend this book to my colleagues who teach Hindi at other US universities. As far as I know, **Let's Learn Hindi** is unique among instructional texts for Hindi.

Professor Ali Asani,
Harvard University
Cambridge, MA, USA

From a physicist and author:

I have spent many years teaching Hindi and have researched all of the books in this field. However, I have found none that compare with **Let's Learn Hindi**, in simplicity and ease of learning. In particular, I find the organization of the book very condusive to learning Hindi quickly.

Glen Kezwer, PhD
India

From a professional educator:

As a professional educator, I am very impressed with Deborah Feinstein's pedagogical approach to learning Hindi. It is practical, easy to use and fun. I have used this book extensively and I would highly recommend it to anyone interested in learning Hindi.

Professor Ellen Rosenberg,
University of British Columbia,
Vancouver, Canada